SPMG

Scottish Heinemann Maths

Textbook

Heinemann

Heinemann Educational Publishers
Halley Court, Jordan Hill, Oxford OX2 8EJ
an imprint of Harcourt Education Ltd

Heinemann is a registered trademark of Harcourt Education Ltd

Writing team
John T Blair
Percy W Farren
John W Thayers
David K Thomson

First Published 2004

08 07 06 05 04 03
10 9 8 7 6 5 4 3 2 1

ISBN 0 435 18002 9

Designed and typeset by Aqua Design Partners.
Illustrated by David Till, David Kearney, Derek Brazell,
Diane Fawcett, Tony O'Donnell, Jon Mitchell, Andy Peters,
James Elston and Aqua Design Partners.
Cover Illustation by James Elston.
Printed and bound by Scotprint, Haddington, East Lothian.

Contents

	TEXTBOOK	EXTENSION TEXTBOOK

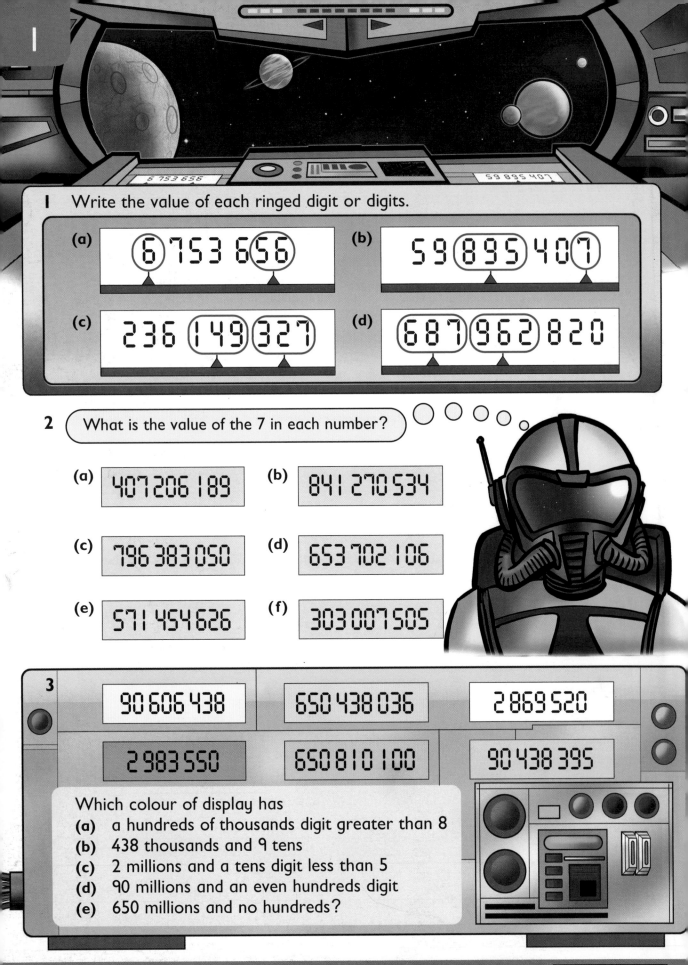

1 Write the value of each ringed digit or digits.

(a) 6 753 656

(b) 59 895 407

(c) 236 149 327

(d) 687 962 820

2 What is the value of the 7 in each number?

(a) 407 206 189

(b) 841 270 534

(c) 796 383 050

(d) 653 702 106

(e) 571 454 626

(f) 303 007 505

3

90 606 438

650 438 036

2 869 520

2 983 550

650 810 100

90 438 395

Which colour of display has
(a) a hundreds of thousands digit greater than 8
(b) 438 thousands and 9 tens
(c) 2 millions and a tens digit less than 5
(d) 90 millions and an even hundreds digit
(e) 650 millions and no hundreds?

Place value: numbers to hundreds of millions

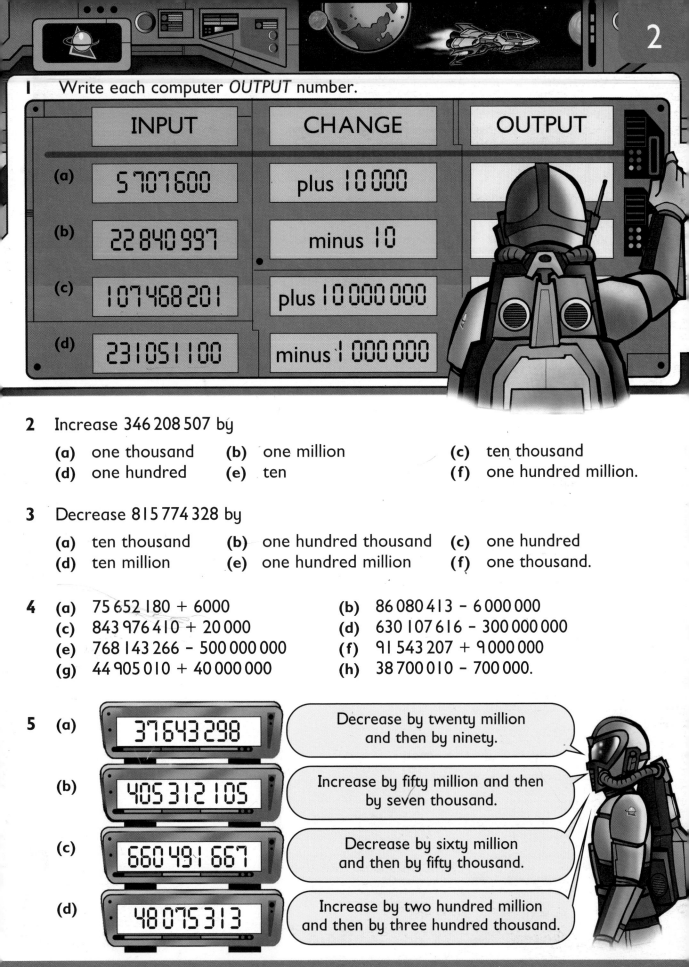

1 Write each computer *OUTPUT* number.

INPUT	CHANGE	OUTPUT
(a) 5 707 600	plus 10 000	
(b) 22 840 997	minus 10	
(c) 107 468 201	plus 10 000 000	
(d) 231 051 100	minus 1 000 000	

2 Increase 346 208 507 by

(a) one thousand　(b) one million　(c) ten thousand
(d) one hundred　(e) ten　(f) one hundred million.

3 Decrease 815 774 328 by

(a) ten thousand　(b) one hundred thousand　(c) one hundred
(d) ten million　(e) one hundred million　(f) one thousand.

4 (a) 75 652 180 + 6000　(b) 86 080 413 − 6 000 000
(c) 843 976 410 + 20 000　(d) 630 107 616 − 300 000 000
(e) 768 143 266 − 500 000 000　(f) 91 543 207 + 9 000 000
(g) 44 905 010 + 40 000 000　(h) 38 700 010 − 700 000.

5 (a) 37 643 298 — Decrease by twenty million and then by ninety.

(b) 405 312 105 — Increase by fifty million and then by seven thousand.

(c) 660 491 667 — Decrease by sixty million and then by fifty thousand.

(d) 48 075 313 — Increase by two hundred million and then by three hundred thousand.

1 Which colour of display shows the lower number?

(a) 8 464 327   8 470 975

(b) 12 501 410   12 500 689

(c) 736 800 400   763 000 505

(d) 919 000 109   909 999 009

2 Which number is (a) lowest (b) highest?

210 840 678   201 574 989   210 840 687

201 547 002   210 840 786   201 745 899

3 List the numbers in order. Start with the smallest.

(a) 121 435 360   112 766 779   121 435 306   112 767 997

(b) 573 654 099   573 654 156   573 654 165   537 685 899

4 Write the number halfway between

(a) 8 000 000 and 9 000 000
(b) 19 000 000 and 20 000 000
(c) 400 000 and 401 000
(d) 200 900 000 and 200 700 000
(e) 38 500 000 and 38 400 000
(f) 10 900 000 and 11 000 000.

5 Write using **numerals**.

(a) Nine million, six hundred and fifty-three thousand.

(b) Twenty-two million sixteen thousand and thirty-one.

(c) Four hundred and sixty-two million, nine thousand and forty.

6 Write in **words**.

(a) 7 850 400   (b) 36 407 010   (c) 563 075 836

I Round to **the nearest thousand** the number shown by each pointer.

2 Round to **the nearest thousand**.

(a)	83 090	(b)	64 499	(c)	75 705	(d)	99 909
(e)	210 805	(f)	323 385	(g)	406 511	(h)	109 269
(i)	519 710	(j)	821 286	(k)	989 747	(l)	991 407

3 Round to **the nearest hundred**.

(a)	62 424	(b)	75 050	(c)	81 663	(d)	89 909
(e)	121 365	(f)	303 510	(g)	761 551	(h)	250 969

4 Round to **the nearest million** the number shown on each gauge.

5 Round to **the nearest million**.

(a)	27 601 310	(b)	35 810 426	(c)	89 409 585
(d)	53 070 999	(e)	71 495 847	(f)	99 505 050
(g)	626 490 850	(h)	200 850 710	(i)	199 356 848
(j)	701 501 005	(k)	311 380 960	(l)	789 511 010

1 Estimate the population of each space colony.

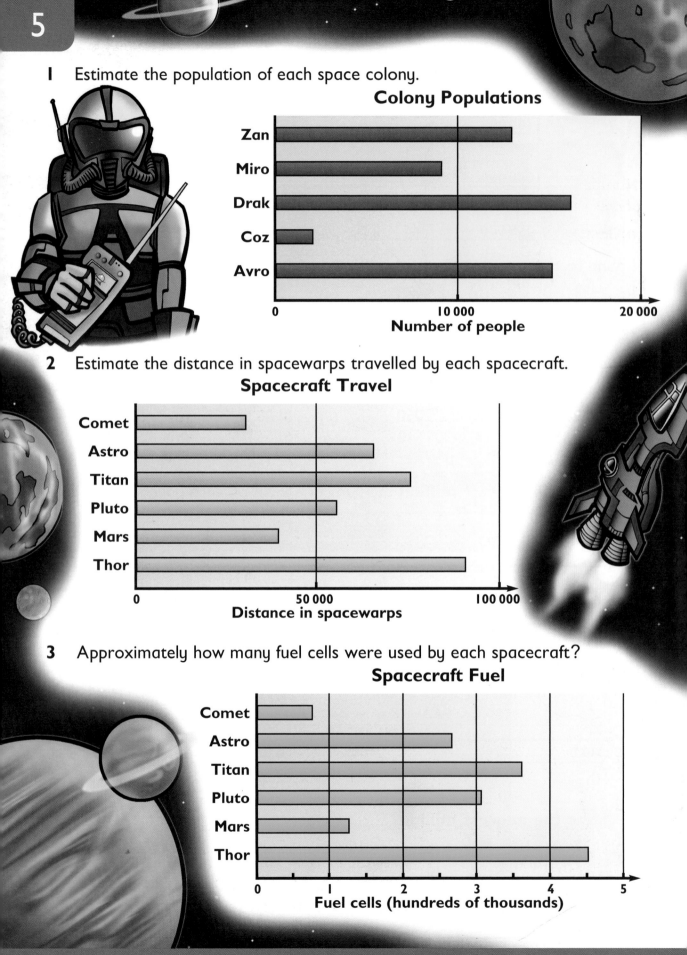

Colony Populations

2 Estimate the distance in spacewarps travelled by each spacecraft.

Spacecraft Travel

3 Approximately how many fuel cells were used by each spacecraft?

Spacecraft Fuel

1 Approximately how many homes on each planet have a computer?

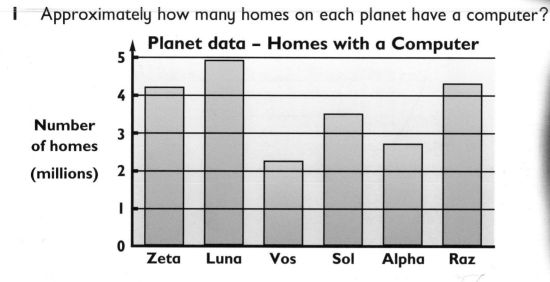

Planet data – Homes with a Computer

Number of homes (millions)

Zeta   Luna   Vos   Sol   Alpha   Raz

2 Estimate the population of each planet.

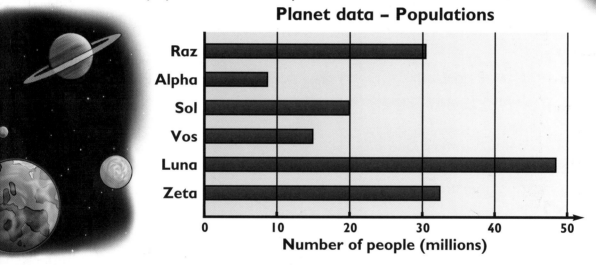

Planet data – Populations

Number of people (millions)

3 Approximately how many video calls were made from each planet?

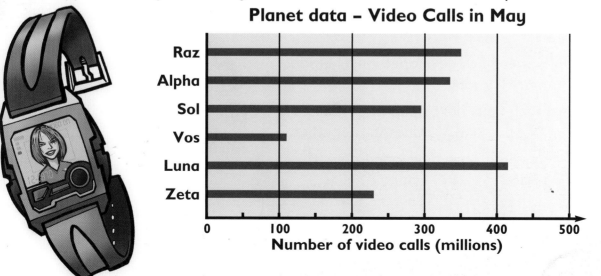

Planet data – Video Calls in May

Number of video calls (millions)

Place value: estimating in millions

CAMERATIX

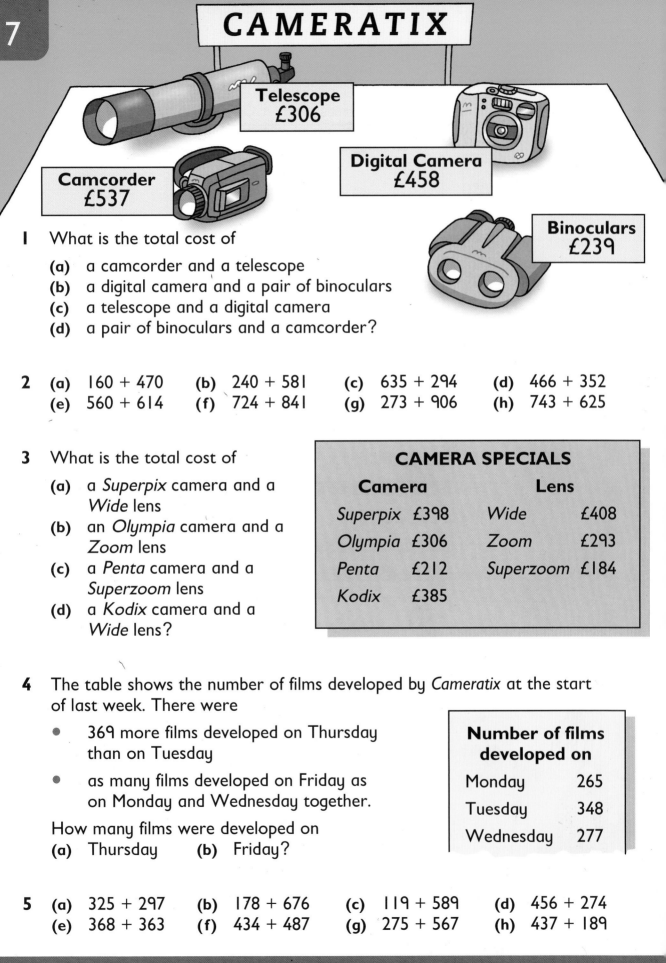

Telescope £306

Digital Camera £458

Camcorder £537

Binoculars £239

1 What is the total cost of

(a) a camcorder and a telescope
(b) a digital camera and a pair of binoculars
(c) a telescope and a digital camera
(d) a pair of binoculars and a camcorder?

2 (a) 160 + 470   (b) 240 + 581   (c) 635 + 294   (d) 466 + 352
    (e) 560 + 614   (f) 724 + 841   (g) 273 + 906   (h) 743 + 625

3 What is the total cost of

(a) a *Superpix* camera and a *Wide* lens
(b) an *Olympia* camera and a *Zoom* lens
(c) a *Penta* camera and a *Superzoom* lens
(d) a *Kodix* camera and a *Wide* lens?

CAMERA SPECIALS

Camera		Lens	
Superpix	£398	Wide	£408
Olympia	£306	Zoom	£293
Penta	£212	Superzoom	£184
Kodix	£385		

4 The table shows the number of films developed by *Cameratix* at the start of last week. There were

- 369 more films developed on Thursday than on Tuesday

- as many films developed on Friday as on Monday and Wednesday together.

How many films were developed on
(a) Thursday   (b) Friday?

Number of films developed on	
Monday	265
Tuesday	348
Wednesday	277

5 (a) 325 + 297   (b) 178 + 676   (c) 119 + 589   (d) 456 + 274
    (e) 368 + 363   (f) 434 + 487   (g) 275 + 567   (h) 437 + 189

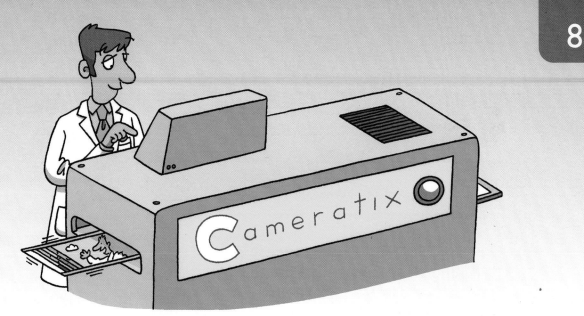

1 The table shows how many digital photographs were printed by *Cameratix* last week.

   Round each number **to the nearest 100** to find the **approximate total** number of photographs printed on

   (a) Monday (b) Tuesday (c) Wednesday
   (d) the mornings only of Monday, Tuesday and Wednesday
   (e) the afternoons only of Monday, Tuesday and Wednesday.

	morning	afternoon
Monday	341	553
Tuesday	667	119
Wednesday	187	694
Thursday	231	578
Friday	492	337
Saturday	715	278

2 Round each number **to the nearest 10** to find the appoximate total number of photographs printed on

   (a) Thursday (b) Friday (c) Saturday
   (d) the mornings only of Thursday, Friday and Saturday
   (e) the afternoons only of Thursday, Friday and Saturday.

3

Daily value of camera/camcorder sales						
	Monday	Tuesday	Wednesday	Thursday	Friday	Saturday
Cameras	£2240	£4876	£7062	£12705	£5217	£5901
Camcorders	£6190	£3928	£2147	£11860	£14192	£19799

Find the approximate total value of cameras and camcorders sold on each day by rounding the values to

   (a) the nearest £1000   (b) the nearest £100.

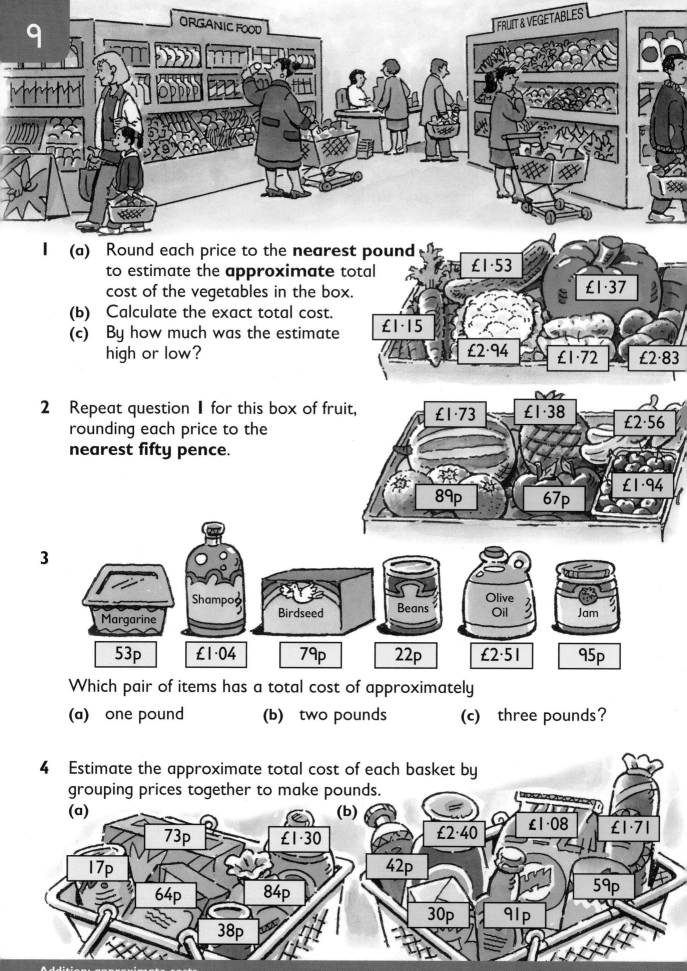

1 (a) Round each price to the **nearest pound** to estimate the **approximate** total cost of the vegetables in the box.

(b) Calculate the exact total cost.

(c) By how much was the estimate high or low?

£1·53

£1·37

£1·15

£2·94

£1·72

£2·83

2 Repeat question 1 for this box of fruit, rounding each price to the **nearest fifty pence**.

£1·73

£1·38

£2·56

£1·94

89p

67p

3

Margarine · 53p

Shampoo · £1·04

Birdseed · 79p

Beans · 22p

Olive Oil · £2·51

Jam · 95p

Which pair of items has a total cost of approximately

(a) one pound   (b) two pounds   (c) three pounds?

4 Estimate the approximate total cost of each basket by grouping prices together to make pounds.

(a)

73p

£1·30

17p

64p

84p

38p

(b)

£2·40

£1·08

£1·71

42p

59p

30p

91p

Addition: approximate costs

1

I estimate my shopping will cost about five pounds.

49p
£1·44
67p
56p
36p
73p
98p

(a) Find the exact total cost.
(b) Which item should be put back to keep the total cost **just under** five pounds?

2

I think my shopping will cost approximately ten pounds.

68p
60p
£2·07
31p
£1·18
£1·56
£2·42
£1·39

(a) Find the exact total cost.
(b) Which item should be put back to keep the total cost **just under** ten pounds?

3 (a) Estimate the total cost of the goods on Sara's list.
(b) Do you think Sara has enough money for the items on her list?
(c) Find the exact total cost.
(d) Suggest an item to remove from the list if Sara does not have enough money.

I have ten pounds to spend.

Sara

sugar	92p
tea	79p
soap-powder	£4·45
toothpaste	£1·23
rice	£2·60
bananas	£1·12

4 Repeat question **3** for • Paul • Carly.

I have twenty pounds to spend.

Paul

lamb	£3·21
plant pot	£2·38
bread	84p
pasta	£1·63
olive oil	£2·36
chicken	£4·15
flowers	£5·59

I only have fifteen pounds.

Carly

potatoes	£1·62
fish	£3·83
ready meal	£3·19
milk	£1·64
shampoo	£2·47
coffee	£2·31
light bulbs	£1·89

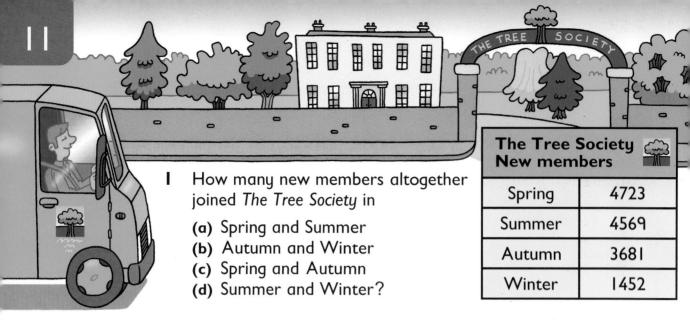

1 How many new members altogether joined *The Tree Society* in

(a) Spring and Summer
(b) Autumn and Winter
(c) Spring and Autumn
(d) Summer and Winter?

The Tree Society New members	
Spring	4723
Summer	4569
Autumn	3681
Winter	1452

2 (a) 9662 + 6089   (b) 6413 + 5795   (c) 4836 + 7217
(d) 3887 + 7494   (e) 5724 + 7598   (f) 3835 + 6786

3 These woodlands are owned by *The Tree Society*. The figures show
● the length in metres of walking trails
● the number of visitors this year.

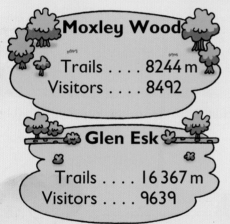

Moxley Wood
Trails . . . . 8244 m
Visitors 8492

Aberfyne Forest
Trails . . . . 27 678 m
Visitors 37 439

Glen Esk
Trails . . . . 16 367 m
Visitors 9639

Fern Estate
Trails . . . . 5816 m
Visitors 23 645

What is the total length of the trails in

(a) Moxley Wood and Glen Esk   (b) Aberfyne Forest and Fern Estate
(c) Moxley Wood and Aberfyne Forest   (d) Fern Estate and Glen Esk?

4 This year, how many people altogether have visited

(a) Moxley Wood and Aberfyne Forest   (b) Glen Esk and Fern Estate
(c) Aberfyne Forest and Glen Esk   (d) Fern Estate and Moxley Wood?

5 (a) 16 314 + 73 + 4835   (b) 7408 + 38 665 + 92
(c) 6704 + 574 + 24 058   (d) 3724 + 103 + 68 + 18 296

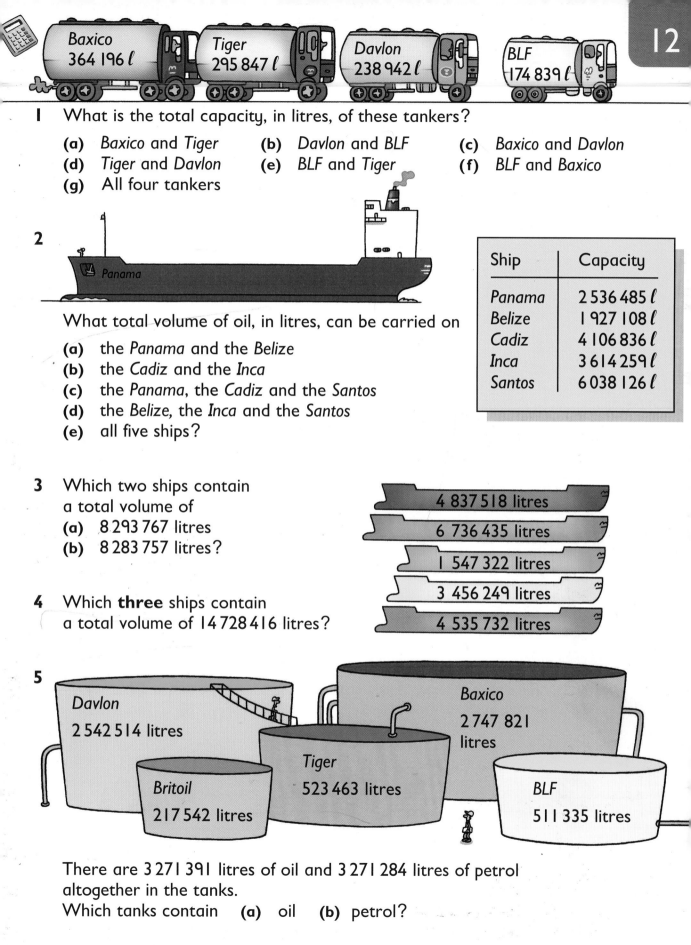

Baxico 364 196 *l*

Tiger 295 847 *l*

Davlon 238 942 *l*

BLF 174 839 *l*

1 What is the total capacity, in litres, of these tankers?

  (a) *Baxico* and *Tiger*   **(b)** *Davlon* and *BLF*   **(c)** *Baxico* and *Davlon*

  (d) *Tiger* and *Davlon*   **(e)** *BLF* and *Tiger*   **(f)** *BLF* and *Baxico*

  (g) All four tankers

2

What total volume of oil, in litres, can be carried on

  (a) the *Panama* and the *Belize*

  (b) the *Cadiz* and the *Inca*

  (c) the *Panama*, the *Cadiz* and the *Santos*

  (d) the *Belize*, the *Inca* and the *Santos*

  (e) all five ships?

Ship	Capacity
Panama	2 536 485 *l*
Belize	1 927 108 *l*
Cadiz	4 106 836 *l*
Inca	3 614 259 *l*
Santos	6 038 126 *l*

3 Which two ships contain a total volume of

  (a) 8 293 767 litres

  (b) 8 283 757 litres?

4 837 518 litres

6 736 435 litres

1 547 322 litres

3 456 249 litres

4 535 732 litres

4 Which **three** ships contain a total volume of 14 728 416 litres?

5

Davlon 2 542 514 litres

Baxico 2 747 821 litres

Tiger 523 463 litres

Britoil 217 542 litres

BLF 511 335 litres

There are 3 271 391 litres of oil and 3 271 284 litres of petrol altogether in the tanks.

Which tanks contain   **(a)** oil   **(b)** petrol?

Green Machine Challenge

1 There is a prize for the vehicle which travels furthest using only 10 ml of fuel. How much further than the white vehicle did the orange vehicle travel?

2 Find the difference, in metres, between these distances travelled:

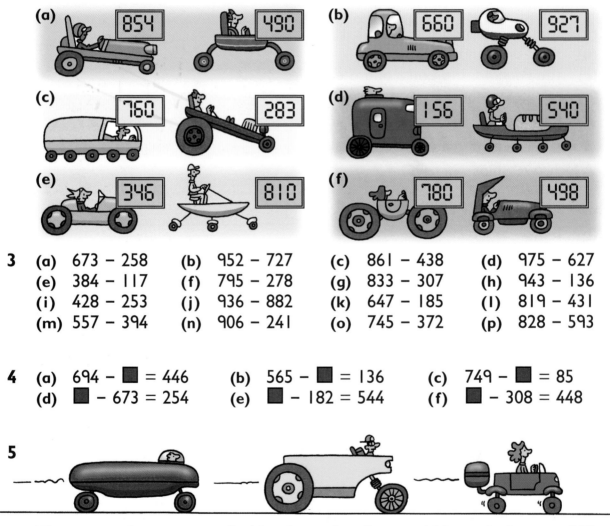

(a) 854 490

(b) 660 927

(c) 760 283

(d) 156 540

(e) 346 810

(f) 780 498

3
(a) 673 – 258	(b) 952 – 727	(c) 861 – 438	(d) 975 – 627
(e) 384 – 117	(f) 795 – 278	(g) 833 – 307	(h) 943 – 136
(i) 428 – 253	(j) 936 – 882	(k) 647 – 185	(l) 819 – 431
(m) 557 – 394	(n) 906 – 241	(o) 745 – 372	(p) 828 – 593

4
(a) 694 – ■ = 446
(b) 565 – ■ = 136
(c) 749 – ■ = 85
(d) ■ – 673 = 254
(e) ■ – 182 = 544
(f) ■ – 308 = 448

5

The **mean** distance travelled by the red, yellow and blue vehicles was 500 m. The blue vehicle travelled 147 m further than the mean and the yellow vehicle travelled 147 m less than the mean.
What distance did each vehicle travel?

1 Use the information in the graph.

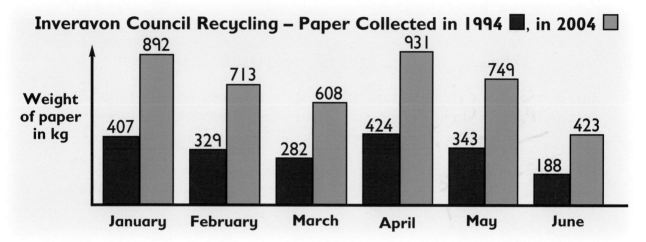

Inveravon Council Recycling – Paper Collected in 1994 ■, in 2004 □

Round each weight **to the nearest 100 kg** to find the **approximate** increase, between 1994 and 2004, in the weight of paper collected during

(a) January   (b) February   (c) March
(d) April   (e) May   (f) June.

2 Round each weight **to the nearest 10 kg** to find, **for 2004**, the approximate difference between the weights of paper collected in

(a) January and February   (b) February and March   (c) March and April
(d) April and May   (e) May and June.

3 *Inveravon Council*

	Weight, in kg, of glass collected for recycling					
	July	August	September	October	November	December
Clear	2190	3792	1081	8207	10 415	12 893
Coloured	3910	6114	4877	11 284	15 299	18 035

Find the approximate difference between the weights of clear and coloured glass collected each month by rounding the weights to

(a) the nearest 1000 kg   (b) the nearest 100 kg.

Woods
9617 m²

Meadow
3503 m²

Loch
6275 m²

Marsh
2549 m²

1 What is the difference between the areas of

    (a) the loch and the meadow   **(b)** the woods and the loch

    (c) the meadow and the marsh   **(d)** the marsh and the woods?

2 **(a)** 4435 − 1478   **(b)** 8702 − 814   **(c)** 5066 − 2189

    (d) 7154 − 3666   **(e)** 9331 − 593   **(f)** 6528 − 2949

3

Trees found in Aberfyne Forest

Larch	14 684
Alder	2831
Fir	22 753
Pine	3492

How many more larch trees are there than

    (a) alder   **(b)** pine?

4 Find the difference between the numbers of fir and

    (a) alder   **(b)** pine.

5 **(a)** 42 675 − 5398   **(b)** 64 230 − 472   **(c)** 23 643 − 7781

    (d) 36 425 − 8768   **(e)** 53 062 − 83   **(f)** 72 027 − 4659

Burndale Country Park Trail Lengths

~~ 14 607 m
8294 m
12 035 m
6528 m

1 Burndale Country Park Rangers collect litter from the walking trails.
What is the total distance walked by Rangers collecting on these trails?

(a) green and yellow   (b) red and yellow

(c) blue, yellow and red   (d) yellow, green and blue

2 How much further do Rangers on the red trail walk than Rangers on

(a) the blue trail   (b) the yellow trail?

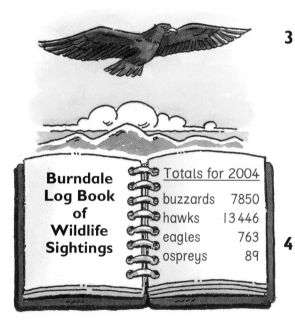

Burndale Log Book of Wildlife Sightings

Totals for 2004

buzzards	7850
hawks	13 446
eagles	763
ospreys	89

3 The Rangers' log book shows the number of wildlife sightings reported by visitors.
In 2004, how many sightings altogether were reported of

(a) hawks and buzzards
(b) ospreys and hawks
(c) hawks and eagles
(d) all four types of bird?

4 How many more sightings were reported of hawks than of

(a) buzzards   (b) eagles   (c) ospreys?

5 (a) 25 915 + 9371   (b) 52 910 − 5372   (c) 175 + 35 719 + 9361

(d) 61 372 − 984   (e) 71 250 − 7904   (f) 9131 + 41 873 + 67

6 In Summer, the number of sightings of deer, red squirrels and hares totalled 13 000.
Together there were 8032 sightings of deer and red squirrels.
The number of sightings of deer was 3156.
How many sightings were reported of

(a) red squirrels   (b) hares?

Burndale Log Book of Wildlife Sightings

Summer Total

red squirrels
deer
hares

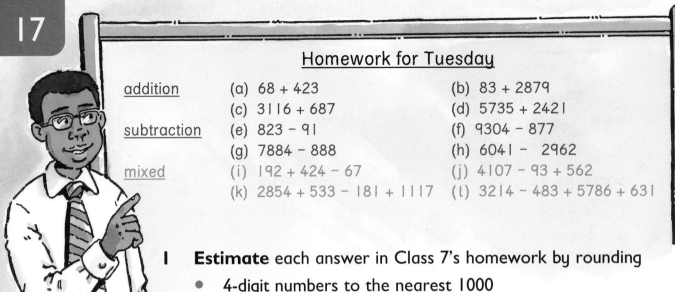

Homework for Tuesday

addition
(a) 68 + 423
(b) 83 + 2879
(c) 3116 + 687
(d) 5735 + 2421

subtraction
(e) 823 – 91
(f) 9304 – 877
(g) 7884 – 888
(h) 6041 – 2962

mixed
(i) 192 + 424 – 67
(j) 4107 – 93 + 562
(k) 2854 + 533 – 181 + 1117
(l) 3214 – 483 + 5786 + 631

1 **Estimate** each answer in Class 7's homework by rounding

- 4-digit numbers to the nearest 1000
- 3-digit numbers to the nearest 100
- 2-digit numbers to the nearest 10.

2 Use your estimated answers in question **1**.
Decide which of Alexa's answers are probably **not** correct.

Alexa

a) 491   b) 2962
c) 3803   d) 7156
e) 732   f) 7427
g) 6996   h) 3079
i) 549   j) 4576
k) 3323   l) 9148

Use Class 7's homework examples.

3 For each addition

- find the **exact** answer
- write a subtraction that can be used to check the answer
- check the answer using the subtraction.

4 Repeat question **3** for each subtraction, this time checking using an addition.

5 For each mixed calculation

- find the **exact** answer
- check the answer by doing the calculation **in a different order**.

6

Ranjit

6335 + 2245

8500 + 35 + 45 → 8580
8000 + 500 + 80 → 8580

Ranjit checks an answer by doing the calculation again **in a different way**.
Show **two** different ways of calculating each of these:

(a) 1728 + 5861 = 7589   (b) 3176 + 6592 = 9768
(c) 9657 – 4484 = 5173   (d) 7040 – 3913 = 3127

1 Serena has collected data about the number of passengers carried by airlines using Newburgh Airport.

Passengers carried by *Aerojet*			
Year	2002	2003	2004
Number	740 128	863 059	1 025 783

How many passengers altogether were carried by *Aerojet* in

(a) 2002 and 2003
(b) 2003 and 2004
(c) all three years?

2 Find the change in the number of passengers carried by *Aerojet* between

(a) 2002 and 2003
(b) 2003 and 2004
(c) 2002 and 2004.

3

Flights in 2004	Number of passengers	
	Domestic	**International**
Scotfly	6 407 275	12 538 607
Aloft	672 430	654 814
Skyhigh	5 295 342	911 961
Easyair	386 596	79 058

In 2004, how many passengers altogether were carried on **Domestic** flights by

(a) *Scotfly* and *Aloft* (b) *Skyhigh* and *Easyair* (c) *Skyhigh* and *Scotfly*
(d) *Aloft* and *Skyhigh* (e) *Easyair* and *Scotfly* (f) *Aloft* and *Easyair*?

4 How many more passengers were carried on **International** flights by *Scotfly* than by

(a) *Aloft* (b) *Skyhigh* (c) *Easyair*?

5 What is the difference between the numbers of passengers carried on Domestic and International flights by each airline?

Alan is checking the stock at the *D.I.Y. WAREHOUSE.*

1 16 large tins of *Shinywhite* gloss paint.

Shinywhite **15** litres

(a) How many litres of *Shinywhite* gloss are there?

(b) 35 × 14 (c) 18 × 25 (d) 45 × 12
(e) 15 × 18 (f) 14 × 45 (g) 16 × 35

2 31 trays of *Mini-candles.*

18 *Mini-candles*

(a) How many *Mini-candles* are there?

(b) 16 × 27 (c) 33 × 12 (d) 14 × 42
(e) 13 × 16 (f) 14 × 38 (g) 46 × 18

3 *Quickbond* **24** sticks

50 boxes of *Quickbond* glue sticks.

(a) How many *Quickbond* glue sticks are there?

(b) 50 × 36 (c) 50 × 48 (d) 50 × 92 (e) 50 × 13
(f) 25 × 28 (g) 25 × 52 (h) 25 × 34 (i) 25 × 19

4

D.I.Y. WAREHOUSE

CHECKED BY: *Alan*

(a) 24 × 23 (b) 21 × 31 (c) 35 × 17
(d) 22 × 28 (e) 27 × 26 (f) 48 × 13
(g) 36 × 21 (h) 11 × 42 (i) 19 × 32

D.I.Y. WAREHOUSE

1 Find the value of these tools held in stock at the *D.I.Y. WAREHOUSE*.

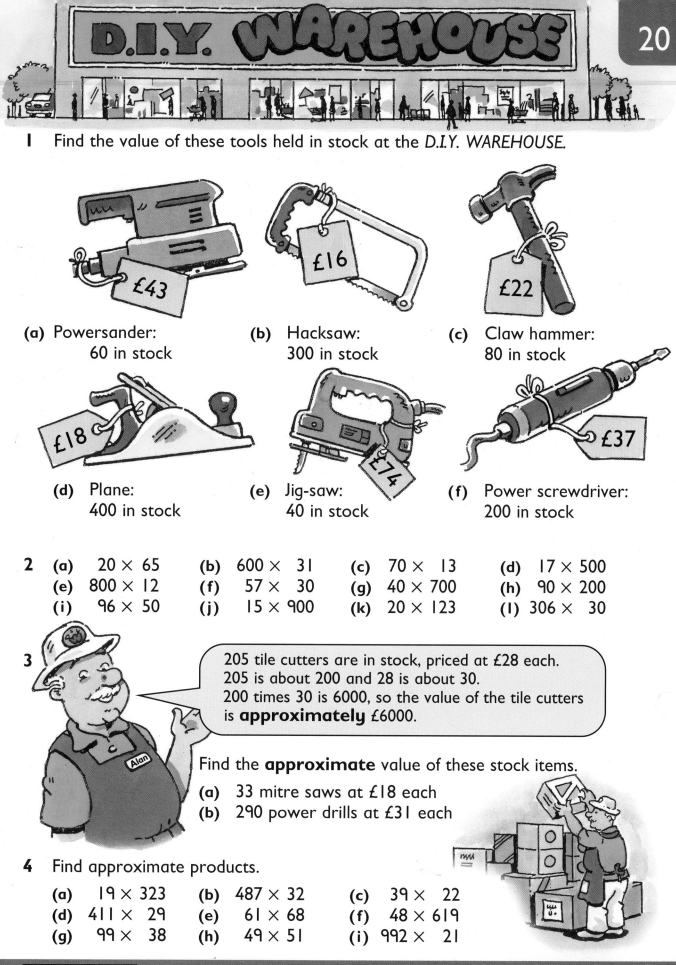

(a) Powersander:
£43
60 in stock

(b) Hacksaw:
£16
300 in stock

(c) Claw hammer:
£22
80 in stock

(d) Plane:
£18
400 in stock

(e) Jig-saw:
£74
40 in stock

(f) Power screwdriver:
£37
200 in stock

2
(a) 20 × 65   (b) 600 × 31   (c) 70 × 13   (d) 17 × 500
(e) 800 × 12   (f) 57 × 30   (g) 40 × 700   (h) 90 × 200
(i) 96 × 50   (j) 15 × 900   (k) 20 × 123   (l) 306 × 30

3

205 tile cutters are in stock, priced at £28 each.
205 is about 200 and 28 is about 30.
200 times 30 is 6000, so the value of the tile cutters is **approximately** £6000.

Find the **approximate** value of these stock items.

(a) 33 mitre saws at £18 each
(b) 290 power drills at £31 each

4 Find approximate products.

(a) 19 × 323   (b) 487 × 32   (c) 39 × 22
(d) 411 × 29   (e) 61 × 68   (f) 48 × 619
(g) 99 × 38   (h) 49 × 51   (i) 992 × 21

HOME ACTIVITY 5   Multiplication: by a multiple of 10/100, approximate products

D.I.Y. WAREHOUSE

New stock needed:

Item	number	cost (each)	total cost
stepladder	100	£17	
wrench	60	£16	
workbench	20	£75	
circular saw	50	£63	
tool set	30	£34	
spade	40	£22	

1 Find the total cost of the

   (a) stepladders   **(b)** wrenches   **(c)** workbenches

   (d) circular saws   **(e)** tool sets   **(f)** spades.

2 How much would *D.I.Y. WAREHOUSE* have to pay for

   (a) 99 stepladders   **(b)** 61 wrenches   **(c)** 19 workbenches

   (d) 51 circular saws   **(e)** 29 tool sets   **(f)** 41 spades

   (g) 22 workbenches   **(h)** 102 stepladders   **(i)** 48 circular saws

   (j) 32 tool sets   **(k)** 58 wrenches   **(l)** 38 spades?

3 **(a)** 101×47 **(b)** 36×49 **(c)** 24×99 **(d)** 51×27

   (e) 19×35 **(f)** 21×43 **(g)** 15×29 **(h)** 41×14

   (i) 23×102 **(j)** 98×26 **(k)** 22×45 **(l)** 52×48

4

> Four hundred and ninety-eight boxes of screws at eleven pounds per box?

Find the answer to Alan's problem.

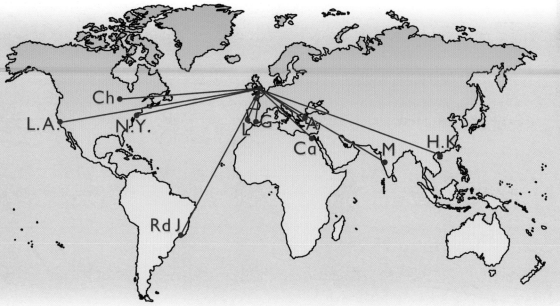

1

Flying distances in kilometres from Newburgh Airport			
Destination	**Distance**	**Destination**	**Distance**
Athens	2878 km	Hong Kong	9645 km
Mumbai	7193 km	Los Angeles	8774 km
Cairo	3519 km	New York	5568 km
Chicago	6356 km	Lisbon	1589 km
Gibraltar	1757 km	Rio de Janeiro	9272 km

Find the total flying distance, in km, of these flights from Newburgh Airport.

(a) 3 flights to Athens (b) 5 flights to Gibraltar (c) 2 flights to Cairo
(d) 4 flights to Lisbon (e) 3 flights to Chicago (f) 2 flights to Rio
(g) 6 flights to New York (h) 4 flights to Hong Kong (i) 5 flights to Mumbai
(j) 7 flights to Los Angeles (k) 8 flights to Athens (l) 9 flights to Chicago

2 (a) 7×4231 (b) 5×7509 (c) 6×3990 (d) 8×8218
(e) 9×5784 (f) 7×9186 (g) 9×4559 (h) 9×7325

3 Last year, once each month from January to June, Ms Smart flew from Newburgh to San Francisco via New York.
She returned each time using the same route in reverse.
The flying distance between New York and San Francisco is 4136 km.

What was Ms Smart's total flying distance on her trips?

Each picture shows:

- the plane's destination
- the number of passengers it can carry.

Majorca 236

Ibiza 275

Malta 78

Rhodes 323

Tenerife 368

Corfu 251

Turkey 294

Cyprus 342

All of the flights are full.

1 Find the total number of people carried to each destination.

(a) 42 flights to Malta
(b) 28 flights to Ibiza
(c) 35 flights to Majorca
(d) 27 flights to Tenerife
(e) 29 flights to Rhodes
(f) 18 flights to Cyprus
(g) 37 flights to Corfu
(h) 33 flights to Turkey

2 A ticket for a flight to Malta costs £127.

What is the total amount collected for one flight?

3 On flights to Cyprus each passenger can take 23 kg of luggage.

Find the total weight of luggage on one flight.

4 Headphones are handed out on flights to Tenerife and Corfu.

How many headphones are handed out on

(a) 38 Tenerife flights
(b) 63 Corfu flights?

1 United agrees to pay a transfer fee in five instalments of £3 435 000. What will the total cost of the transfer be?

Now 25p

Daily Post

Bigcity United sign Brazilian ace Perez

This week Bigcity signed the Perez will be. Dispite rumors that head had lost a leg last summer

2

Pop in the Park

Altogether, 43 297 tickets, each costing £49, are sold for *Pop in the Park*. What is the total value of the ticket sales?

3 National Lottery grants, each for £1 732 950, are given to eleven art galleries and museums around Britain. How much money altogether is given in grants?

THE ART GALLERY

4

Last year, *Marsden Self-Build* sold 148 of their *Belmont* kit houses. Each house cost £48 265. What was the total value of these sales?

5 **Investigate**. About how many **minutes** do you spend
  ● sleeping   ● watching television   ● at school
  (a) in a day   **(b)** in a week   **(c)** in a year?

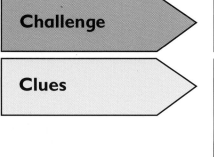

| Challenge | What number multiplied by itself gives a product of 1 522 756? |

| Clues | The number
● has 4 digits, all of which are different
● is even
● has a digit sum of 10
● has a difference of 3 between the first and last digits. |

1 Paperback books are shared equally among shelves.
How many books are on each shelf?

   (a) 2800 fiction books   **(b)** 1800 non-fiction books   **(c)** 4500 children's books

    on 7 shelves   on 6 shelves   on 9 shelves

2 **(a)** $2400 \div 4$ **(b)** $6400 \div 8$ **(c)** $3500 \div 5$ **(d)** $2700 \div 3$
    (e) $7200 \div 9$ **(f)** $5600 \div 7$ **(g)** $4200 \div 6$ **(h)** $3600 \div 4$
    (i) $4900 \div \blacksquare = 700$ **(j)** $5400 \div \blacksquare = 900$ **(k)** $3200 \div \blacksquare = 400$

3 Seventy-four antique books are divided equally among six display cases.

How many books are in each case and how many are left over?

4 **(a)** $53 \div 4$ **(b)** $79 \div 7$ **(c)** $42 \div 3$ **(d)** $111 \div 9$ **(e)** $100 \div 8$

5

Three thousand six hundred bookmarks are shared equally among three boxes.
How many bookmarks are in each box?

6 **(a)** $8400 \div 4$ **(b)** $3550 \div 5$ **(c)** $4260 \div 6$ **(d)** $7290 \div 9$
    (e) $2480 \div 8$ **(f)** $2170 \div 7$ **(g)** $3280 \div 4$ **(h)** $1890 \div 3$
    (i) $4008 \div 8$ **(j)** $2721 \div 3$ **(k)** $2545 \div 5$ **(l)** $3618 \div 6$

1 Tickets for Inveravon Thistle's cup tie are divided equally among boxes.

How many tickets are in each box?

(a) 8813 North Stand tickets in 7 boxes
(b) 4116 Family Enclosure tickets in 3 boxes
(c) 9171 Main Stand tickets in 9 boxes
(d) 6235 Visitors Enclosure tickets in 5 boxes

Quarter-final tie
INVERAVON THISTLE
versus
Newburgh Rovers
Main Stand, Section C
Row FF, Seat 32

2 (a) 8276 ÷ 4 (b) 9474 ÷ 6 (c) 7496 ÷ 8 (d) 7526 ÷ 5 (e) 6041 ÷ 3
(f) 5109 ÷ 2 (g) 7823 ÷ 5 (h) 9088 ÷ 9 (i) 9623 ÷ 3 (j) 8695 ÷ 4

3 The 16 650 match programmes have been distributed equally among 9 sales booths.

How many programmes are in each booth?

4 A supply of 36 480 napkins has been divided equally among 8 refreshment kiosks.

How many napkins are in each kiosk?

5 (a) 28 188 ÷ 6 (b) 30 772 ÷ 4 (c) 17 942 ÷ 2 (d) 21 702 ÷ 3
(e) 43 567 ÷ 5 (f) 10 425 ÷ 7 (g) 50 384 ÷ 4 (h) 79 234 ÷ 6

1   Jake and Billy are paid the same
    weekly rate for their work as builders.
    Jake works for six weeks and Billy
    works for two weeks on the same job.
    Their total pay is £4768.

    How much does each receive?

2.  Nine tins of beans weigh 4 kg 860 g altogether.

    (a)   What is the weight of seven tins?
    (b)   How many tins together weigh 2 kg 160 g?

    Each tin of beans is 7 cm tall.

    (c)   How many layers can be stacked in a
          cupboard with a height of 1 m 3 cm?

3   A set of 5 numbers has a **range**
    of 660. The hidden number is also
    the **largest.**

    Find
    (a)   the hidden number
    (b)   the **mean** of the set
          of 5 numbers.

1760   1530   1940   1880

4   Copy and complete each number chain.

    (a) | 8400 | ÷ 4 | | + 35 | | ÷ 7 | | ÷ 5 | |

    (b) | 9045 | ÷ 9 | | ÷ 5 | | + 43 | | ÷ 4 | |

5   (a)   Which of these multiplications give a product that
          is exactly divisible by 6?

    1 × 3 × 5   2 × 3 × 4   2 × 8 × 10   5 × 6 × 7   3 × 7 × 9   8 × 9 × 10

    (b)   What do you notice about the numbers in your answer to (a)?
    (c)   Check to see if what you noticed is true for other multiplications like these.

1 Emergency sacks of food are divided equally among crates.
How many sacks are in each crate?

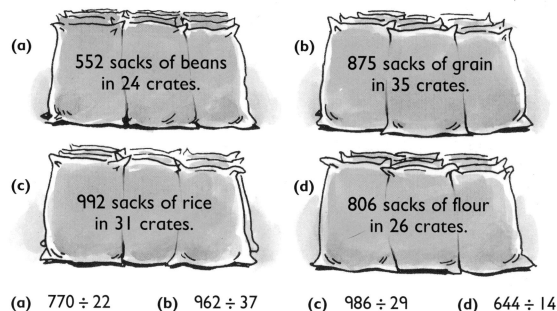

(a) 552 sacks of beans in 24 crates.

(b) 875 sacks of grain in 35 crates.

(c) 992 sacks of rice in 31 crates.

(d) 806 sacks of flour in 26 crates.

2 **(a)** $770 \div 22$ **(b)** $962 \div 37$ **(c)** $986 \div 29$ **(d)** $644 \div 14$

3 Medical items are shared equally among boxes.
How many items are in each box and how many are left over?

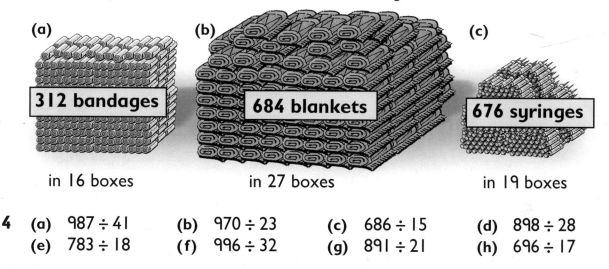

(a) **312 bandages** in 16 boxes

(b) **684 blankets** in 27 boxes

(c) **676 syringes** in 19 boxes

4 **(a)** $987 \div 41$ **(b)** $970 \div 23$ **(c)** $686 \div 15$ **(d)** $898 \div 28$
  (e) $783 \div 18$ **(f)** $996 \div 32$ **(g)** $891 \div 21$ **(h)** $696 \div 17$

Division: a three-digit number by a two-digit number, including remainders

Forty-three.

1 Salma and Conor both have the same answer to **516 ÷ 12**.

Salma checks her answer using **factors**.

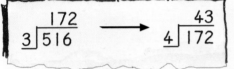

$$3\overline{)516} = 172 \longrightarrow 4\overline{)172} = 43$$

Conor checks by **multiplying**.

$$\begin{array}{r} 43 \\ \times 12 \\ \hline 86 \\ 430 \\ \hline 516 \end{array}$$

Check your answers to these divisions using

● Salma's method ● Conor's method.

(a) 432 ÷ 16 **(b)** 864 ÷ 24 **(c)** 728 ÷ 28 **(d)** 918 ÷ 27

2 Without calculating, copy and complete each number statement using ☒ or ☷ or ☐ or ☐.

(a) 962 ☐ 37 = 26 **(b)** 33 ☐ 29 = 957 **(c)** 966 ☐ 23 = 42
(d) 957 ☐ 33 = 990 **(e)** 966 ☐ 42 = 924 **(f)** 37 ☐ 26 = 63
(g) 42 ☐ 23 = 966 **(h)** 962 ☐ 26 = 37 **(i)** 957 ☐ 33 = 29

3 Eric and Mae have **different** answers to **819 ÷ 39**.

Eric explains why he thinks he is correct.

819 divided by 39 is approximately 800 divided by 40, which gives 20.

Use Eric's method to check these divisions. Explain, for each, why you **think** it is correct or incorrect.

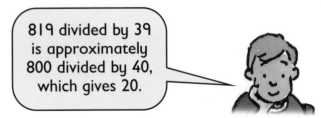

(a) 608 ÷ 19 = 32
(b) 891 ÷ 27 = 23
(c) 504 ÷ 21 = 33
(d) 429 ÷ 39 = 11

NATIONAL FUND FOR THE ARTS

1

The three main museums in Rockburgh are **each** given grants of £10650.
The city of Bexham is given £32970 to be shared equally among fourteen small galleries.

Rockburgh

Bexham

(a) Which city receives the larger amount and by how much?

(b) What is the difference between the grants given to a museum and to a gallery?

2 The total grant given to twelve drama groups is double the total grant given to eight writers' workshops.
Each workshop receives £1920.
How much does each drama group receive?

3

A total amount of £15525000 is shared equally among nine regions.
Each region puts 50% of its amount into a reserve fund.
Northern Region distributes the rest equally among fifteen local projects.

(a) How much does each region receive?

(b) What is the total amount put into reserve funds?

(c) How much is given to each project in Northern Region?

WITH THE HELP OF A GRANT FROM THE NATIONAL FUND FOR THE ARTS.

1 What number is on the skittle that does not belong to the set?

Set A: multiples of 3   **Set B: multiples of 4**   **Set C: multiples of 5**

2 List the skittle numbers from question **1** that are **common multiples** of

(a) 3 and 4   (b) 3 and 5   (c) 4 and 5.

3 Write the **smallest** number that is a common multiple of

(a) 3 and 7   (b) 8 and 5   (c) 3 and 12   (d) 28 and 4

(e) 8 and 10   (f) 10 and 35   (g) 12 and 21   (h) 56 and 21

4

The rule for my number sequence is **multiply by 3** each time.

1, 3, 9, 27, 81, 243, 729, 2187

List the **first eight** terms in each number sequence and write the rule.

(a) 7, 20, 33, 46, ...   (b) 115, 99, 83, 67, ...
(c) 4, 55, 106, 157, ...   (d) 351, 302, 253, 204, ...
(e) 219, 188, 157, 126, ...   (f) 6, 35, 64, 93, ...
(g) 1·09, 1·34, 1·59, 1·84, ... (h) 2187, 729, 243, 81, ...

5 Copy and complete each number sequence.
(a) 3, 6, 12, ■, ■, 96   (b) 678, ■, 456, 345, ■, 123
(c) ■, ■, 7, 13, 21, 31   (d) ■, 81, 64, ■, 36, 25
(e) 2, 3, 5, 8, 13, ■, 34   (f) 1, 1, 2, 6, 24, ■, 720

1 Stanley arranges displays of
   items for sale in a supermarket.
   (a) How many boxes are in
        each of these four stacks?

   (b) Draw the fifth and sixth stacks in Stanley's pattern.
        How many boxes are in each stack?
   (c) **Without** drawing stacks, write the number of boxes in
        the seventh and eighth stacks.
   (d) How can you calculate the number of boxes in the ninth stack?

   (e) The stacks of boxes are triangular shaped.
        The numbers 1, 3, 6, 10, ... and so on
        are called **triangular numbers.**

        List the triangular numbers from 1 to 120.

2 (a) Stanley puts his second and
        third stacks together like this:
        Draw pairs of consecutive stacks
        put together in the same way.

   (b) Add pairs of consecutive triangular numbers.
        What type of number is each total?

3 (a) Which triangular numbers less than 100 are also square numbers?
   (b) Make 100 by adding
        • two triangular numbers   • three triangular numbers.

1 Write these temperatures in order.
- Start with the **lowest**.
  - **(a)** 6°C, ⁻2°C, 10°C, ⁻5°C, ⁻10°C
  - **(b)** ⁻4°C, 7°C, 0°C, ⁻8°C, 3°C
- Start with the **highest**.
  - **(c)** ⁻27°C, 1°C, 26°C, ⁻1°C, ⁻14°C
  - **(d)** ⁻34°C, ⁻2°C, 2°C, ⁻43°C, 24°C

2 **(a)** What temperature is shown by the thermometer?
(b) What will the temperature be after it falls by 15 degrees?

3 What is the new temperature after a temperature of 6°C

(a) rises by 7 degrees
(b) falls by 4 degrees
(c) falls by 6 degrees
(d) falls by 26 degrees?

4 What is the new temperature after a temperature of ⁻11°C

(a) falls by 3 degrees
(b) rises by 3 degrees
(c) falls by 11 degrees
(d) rises by 22 degrees?

5 Find, in degrees, the difference between temperatures of

(a) 16°C and ⁻2°C   (b) 4°C and ⁻32°C   (c) ⁻5°C and ⁻35°C.

°C
25°
15°
5°
0
⁻5°
⁻15°
⁻25°
⁻35°

6 The normal water level in a swimming pool should be 2 metres.
Sally keeps a record of the water level, **in centimetres**, above or below normal, like this:

Mon	Tue	Wed	Thu	Fri	Sat
+4	+2	⁻3	⁻5	0	⁻4

Write the water level for each day.

7 **(a)** List all the different pairs of whole numbers which have a total of 6.
(b) Find pairs of numbers, **one of which is negative**, which total 6.

$$5 + 1 = 6$$
$$4 + 2 = 6$$
$$3 +$$

Canoes for hire

20 42 45 54 63 72 90 96

1 Which canoe numbers have as a factor
  (a) 2 (b) 3 (c) 5 (d) 9?

2 (a) Copy and complete this table for numbers **from 1 to 20**.

Number	Factors	Number of factors
1	1	1
2	1, 2	2
3	1, 3	2
4	1, 2, 4	3

  (b) What type of number has
   ● an **odd** number of factors ● **only two** factors?

3 Which of these are **prime numbers**?

31 41 51 61

4 (a) List all the factors of 24.
  (b) Which factors of 24 are prime numbers?
  (c) Use only **prime factors** of 24 to write a multiplication with a product of 24.

$24 = 2 \times 2$

5 Use only prime factors of each number to write multiplications with products of

  (a) (b) (c) (d)

12 30 36 63

Seasalt Boating

Seasalt Boating

Mermaid	£3272
Seagull	£6536
Seaspray	£7650
Shark	£20 160
Seacat	£9824
Gannet	£1908

Boat Prices

Seafoam	£33 836
Neptune	£8352
Seashell	£5488
Puffin	£41 792
Seahorse	£4572
Seashanty	£17 616

1 (a) Which of the boat prices are exactly divisible by 8?

(b) Copy and complete.

Prices (£s) exactly divisible by 8	3272						
Last 3 digits of the price	272						
Are the last 3 digits exactly divisible by 8?	Yes						

(c) Describe how you can check that a number is exactly divisible by 8.

2 (a) Which of these prices at *Seasalt Boating* are exactly divisible by 9?

| £9855 | £6804 | £2080 | £87 246 | £47 849 | £6531 | £1422 |

| £58 463 | £2997 | £14 170 | £7362 | £5179 | £34 731 | £969 318 |

(b) Copy and complete.

Prices (£s) exactly divisible by 9	9855						
Sum of the digits in the price	27						
Is the digit sum exactly divisible by 9?	Yes						

(c) Describe how you can check that a number is exactly divisible by 9.

3 Which of these numbers are

- exactly divisible by 8
- not exactly divisible by 9?

   8856   24 632   3564   59 904   32 178   7424

1 Copy and complete

(a) the table: for the number of wheels on buggies

(b) the rule: the number of wheels is ____ times the number of buggies

(c) the formula: **W** = ____ × **B**

Number of buggies (B)	Number of wheels (W)
1	4.
2	
3	
4	
5	

2 A new fuel additive called *Energen* is being tested on the buggies.

Copy and complete

(a) the table: for adding capsules of *Energen*

(b) the rule: the number of capsules is ____ more than the number of litres

(c) the formula: **C** = **L** + ____

Add one capsule of *Energen* for each litre of fuel, then add two more capsules.

Number of litres (L)	Number of capsules (C)
1	3
2	
3	
4	
5	

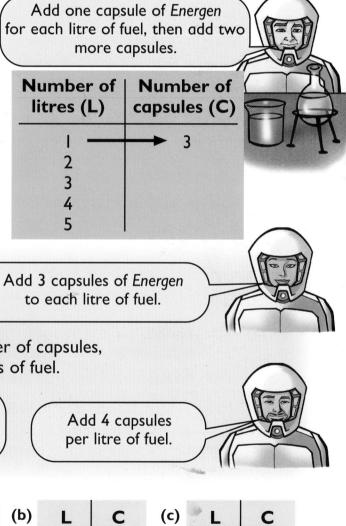

3 For each of these experiments

(a) make a table

(b) write a rule, in words, for finding the number of capsules

(c) write a formula for **C**, the number of capsules, which uses **L**, the number of litres of fuel.

Add 3 capsules of *Energen* to each litre of fuel.

Add one capsule for each litre of fuel, then add 5 more capsules.

Add 4 capsules per litre of fuel.

4 For each table, write a formula for **C**, using **L**.

C = ⬚

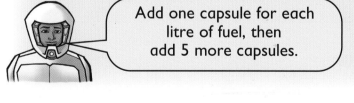

(a)

L	C
1	11
2	12
3	13
4	14

(b)

L	C
2	1
4	2
6	3
8	4

(c)

L	C
6	3
7	4
8	5
9	6

1 A buggy weighs 5 kilograms. Fuel flasks weigh 1 kilogram each.

(a) Copy and complete the table to show the total weight when a buggy has 1, 2, 3, ...6 fuel flasks.

(b) Which formula is correct?

Number of fuel flasks (F)	Weight (W) in kg of buggy + fuel flasks
1	6
2	
3	

$W = 5 \times F$ $W = F + 5$ $W = F - 5$

(c) Use the formula to find the total weight when there are
- 8 fuel flasks
- 10 fuel flasks
- 15 fuel flasks
- 17 fuel flasks.

2 (a) Each 8 kg of moonrock mined by buggies contains 1 kg of talium crystals. What weight of talium is contained in each of these piles of moonrock?

64 kg

40 kg   **88 kg**

(b) Write a formula for **T**, the weight of talium crystals contained in **M** kilograms of moonrock.

(c) Use your formula to find **T** when
- **M** = 160 kg
- **M** = 56 kg
- **M** = 3200 kg

3 The formula $D = 5 \times T$ gives the depth **D**, in metres, drilled by a buggy in **T** hours.

Use the formula to find the depth drilled by a buggy in
(a) 4 hours   (b) 7 hours   (c) $\frac{1}{2}$ hour   (d) $1\frac{1}{2}$ hours.

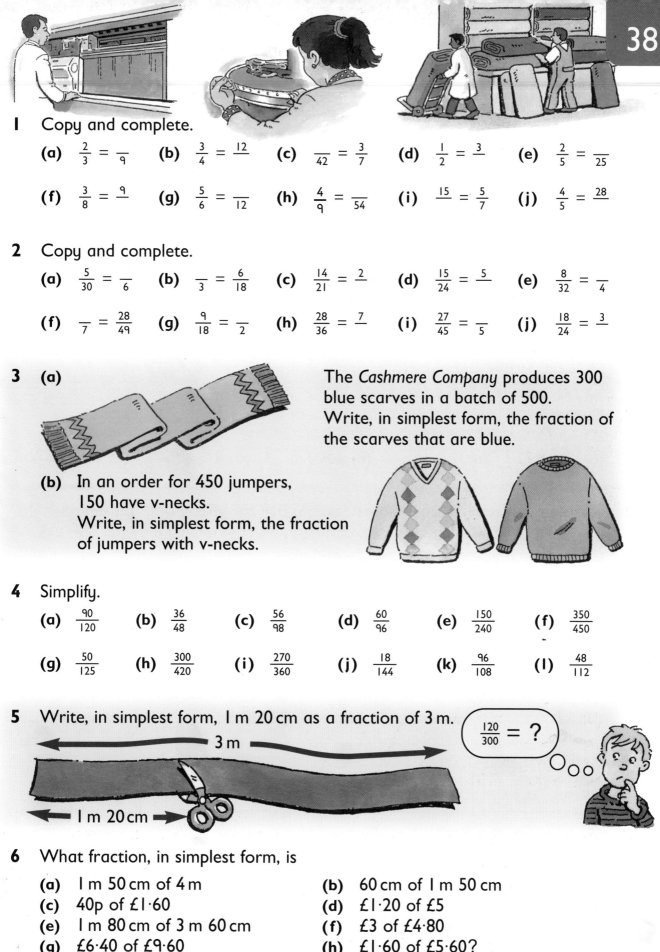

1 Copy and complete.

(a) $\frac{2}{3} = \frac{}{9}$ (b) $\frac{3}{4} = \frac{12}{}$ (c) $\frac{}{42} = \frac{3}{7}$ (d) $\frac{1}{2} = \frac{3}{}$ (e) $\frac{2}{5} = \frac{}{25}$

(f) $\frac{3}{8} = \frac{9}{}$ (g) $\frac{5}{6} = \frac{}{12}$ (h) $\frac{4}{9} = \frac{}{54}$ (i) $\frac{15}{} = \frac{5}{7}$ (j) $\frac{4}{5} = \frac{28}{}$

2 Copy and complete.

(a) $\frac{5}{30} = \frac{}{6}$ (b) $\frac{}{3} = \frac{6}{18}$ (c) $\frac{14}{21} = \frac{2}{}$ (d) $\frac{15}{24} = \frac{5}{}$ (e) $\frac{8}{32} = \frac{}{4}$

(f) $\frac{}{7} = \frac{28}{49}$ (g) $\frac{9}{18} = \frac{}{2}$ (h) $\frac{28}{36} = \frac{7}{}$ (i) $\frac{27}{45} = \frac{}{5}$ (j) $\frac{18}{24} = \frac{3}{}$

3 (a) The *Cashmere Company* produces 300 blue scarves in a batch of 500.
Write, in simplest form, the fraction of the scarves that are blue.

(b) In an order for 450 jumpers, 150 have v-necks.
Write, in simplest form, the fraction of jumpers with v-necks.

4 Simplify.

(a) $\frac{90}{120}$ (b) $\frac{36}{48}$ (c) $\frac{56}{98}$ (d) $\frac{60}{96}$ (e) $\frac{150}{240}$ (f) $\frac{350}{450}$

(g) $\frac{50}{125}$ (h) $\frac{300}{420}$ (i) $\frac{270}{360}$ (j) $\frac{18}{144}$ (k) $\frac{96}{108}$ (l) $\frac{48}{112}$

5 Write, in simplest form, 1 m 20 cm as a fraction of 3 m.

$\frac{120}{300} = ?$

3 m

1 m 20 cm

6 What fraction, in simplest form, is

(a) 1 m 50 cm of 4 m (b) 60 cm of 1 m 50 cm

(c) 40p of £1·60 (d) £1·20 of £5

(e) 1 m 80 cm of 3 m 60 cm (f) £3 of £4·80

(g) £6·40 of £9·60 (h) £1·60 of £5·60?

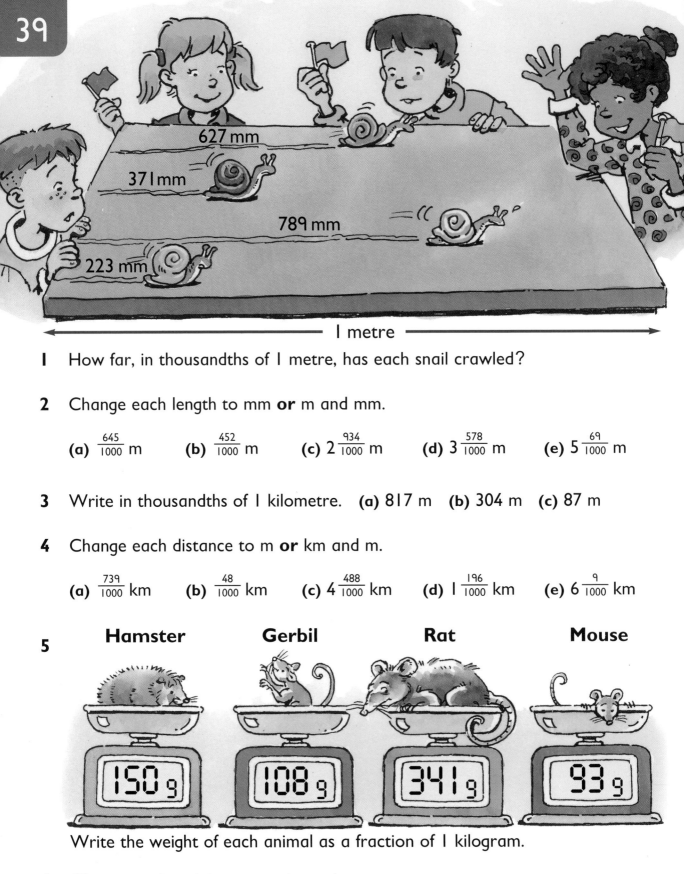

627 mm

371 mm

789 mm

223 mm

|← 1 metre →|

1 How far, in thousandths of 1 metre, has each snail crawled?

2 Change each length to mm **or** m and mm.

(a) $\frac{645}{1000}$ m (b) $\frac{452}{1000}$ m (c) $2\frac{934}{1000}$ m (d) $3\frac{578}{1000}$ m (e) $5\frac{69}{1000}$ m

3 Write in thousandths of 1 kilometre. (a) 817 m (b) 304 m (c) 87 m

4 Change each distance to m **or** km and m.

(a) $\frac{739}{1000}$ km (b) $\frac{48}{1000}$ km (c) $4\frac{488}{1000}$ km (d) $1\frac{196}{1000}$ km (e) $6\frac{9}{1000}$ km

5

Hamster	Gerbil	Rat	Mouse
150 g	108 g	341 g	93 g

Write the weight of each animal as a fraction of 1 kilogram.

6 Change each weight to g **or** kg and g.

(a) $\frac{764}{1000}$ kg (b) $\frac{22}{1000}$ kg (c) $3\frac{999}{1000}$ kg (d) $7\frac{866}{1000}$ kg (e) $2\frac{7}{1000}$ kg

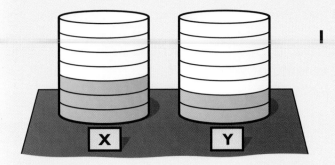

1 The capacity of each jar is 1 litre.

(a) What volume of water, in ℓ, is in
 • jar **X** • jar **Y**?

(b) What volume, in ℓ, is in jar **Y** after the contents of jar **X** have been poured into it?

2 (a) $\frac{5}{7} + \frac{1}{7}$ (b) $\frac{2}{9} + \frac{6}{9}$ (c) $\frac{1}{5} + \frac{3}{5}$ (d) $\frac{2}{10} + \frac{7}{10}$

  (e) $\frac{3}{8} + \frac{4}{8}$ (f) $\frac{1}{6} + \frac{2}{6}$ (g) $\frac{5}{8} + \frac{1}{8}$ (h) $\frac{4}{9} + \frac{2}{9}$

3 The diagram shows the addition
   $1\frac{3}{10} \quad \frac{4}{10} = 1\frac{7}{10}$

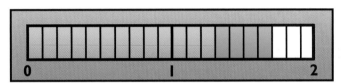

Write an addition for each of these diagrams.

(a)

(b)

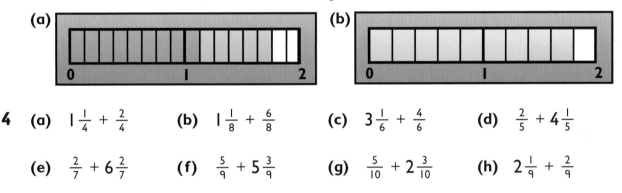

4 (a) $1\frac{1}{4} + \frac{2}{4}$ (b) $1\frac{1}{8} + \frac{6}{8}$ (c) $3\frac{1}{6} + \frac{4}{6}$ (d) $\frac{2}{5} + 4\frac{1}{5}$

  (e) $\frac{2}{7} + 6\frac{2}{7}$ (f) $\frac{5}{9} + 5\frac{3}{9}$ (g) $\frac{5}{10} + 2\frac{3}{10}$ (h) $2\frac{1}{9} + \frac{2}{9}$

5 Write an addition to show the total length, in m, of these two coloured strips.

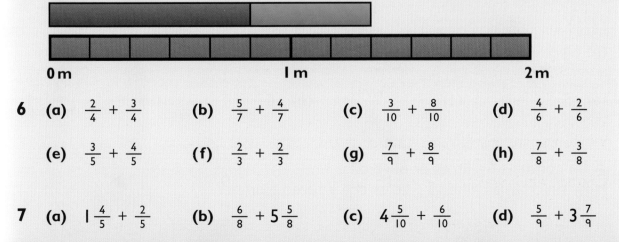

6 (a) $\frac{2}{4} + \frac{3}{4}$ (b) $\frac{5}{7} + \frac{4}{7}$ (c) $\frac{3}{10} + \frac{8}{10}$ (d) $\frac{4}{6} + \frac{2}{6}$

  (e) $\frac{3}{5} + \frac{4}{5}$ (f) $\frac{2}{3} + \frac{2}{3}$ (g) $\frac{7}{9} + \frac{8}{9}$ (h) $\frac{7}{8} + \frac{3}{8}$

7 (a) $1\frac{4}{5} + \frac{2}{5}$ (b) $\frac{6}{8} + 5\frac{5}{8}$ (c) $4\frac{5}{10} + \frac{6}{10}$ (d) $\frac{5}{9} + 3\frac{7}{9}$

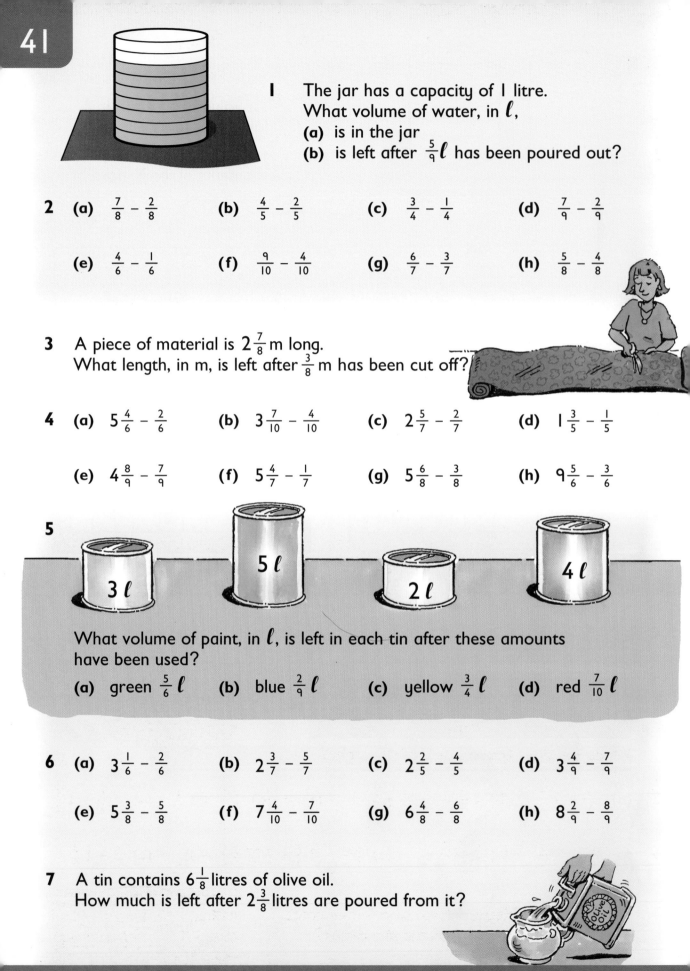

1 The jar has a capacity of 1 litre.
What volume of water, in ℓ,
(a) is in the jar
(b) is left after $\frac{5}{9}\ell$ has been poured out?

2 (a) $\frac{7}{8} - \frac{2}{8}$ (b) $\frac{4}{5} - \frac{2}{5}$ (c) $\frac{3}{4} - \frac{1}{4}$ (d) $\frac{7}{9} - \frac{2}{9}$

(e) $\frac{4}{6} - \frac{1}{6}$ (f) $\frac{9}{10} - \frac{4}{10}$ (g) $\frac{6}{7} - \frac{3}{7}$ (h) $\frac{5}{8} - \frac{4}{8}$

3 A piece of material is $2\frac{7}{8}$ m long.
What length, in m, is left after $\frac{3}{8}$ m has been cut off?

4 (a) $5\frac{4}{6} - \frac{2}{6}$ (b) $3\frac{7}{10} - \frac{4}{10}$ (c) $2\frac{5}{7} - \frac{2}{7}$ (d) $1\frac{3}{5} - \frac{1}{5}$

(e) $4\frac{8}{9} - \frac{7}{9}$ (f) $5\frac{4}{7} - \frac{1}{7}$ (g) $5\frac{6}{8} - \frac{3}{8}$ (h) $9\frac{5}{6} - \frac{3}{6}$

5

What volume of paint, in ℓ, is left in each tin after these amounts have been used?
(a) green $\frac{5}{6}\ell$ (b) blue $\frac{2}{9}\ell$ (c) yellow $\frac{3}{4}\ell$ (d) red $\frac{7}{10}\ell$

6 (a) $3\frac{1}{6} - \frac{2}{6}$ (b) $2\frac{3}{7} - \frac{5}{7}$ (c) $2\frac{2}{5} - \frac{4}{5}$ (d) $3\frac{4}{9} - \frac{7}{9}$

(e) $5\frac{3}{8} - \frac{5}{8}$ (f) $7\frac{4}{10} - \frac{7}{10}$ (g) $6\frac{4}{8} - \frac{6}{8}$ (h) $8\frac{2}{9} - \frac{8}{9}$

7 A tin contains $6\frac{1}{8}$ litres of olive oil.
How much is left after $2\frac{3}{8}$ litres are poured from it?

1 Find the total amount of pizza each customer has ordered.

Ahmed Alana George David Kim Laura

2 How much more pizza has been ordered by

(a) Ahmed than Alana   (b) David than George
(c) David than Ahmed   (d) George than Alana
(e) Laura than Alana   (f) Laura than Ahmed?

3 How much pizza altogether has been ordered by

(a) Ahmed and George   (b) Alana and David
(c) David and Ahmed   (d) Kim and Laura?

4

Garlic Bread - sold by the metre.

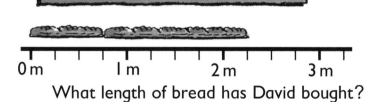

0 m   1 m   2 m   3 m

What length of bread has David bought?

5 (a) $\frac{1}{4} + 1\frac{1}{2}$ (b) $1\frac{1}{4} + \frac{3}{4}$ (c) $\frac{3}{4} + 1\frac{3}{4}$ (d) $1\frac{1}{4} + 1\frac{1}{2}$ (e) $1\frac{3}{4} + 1\frac{1}{2}$

6 (a) $1\frac{1}{2} - \frac{1}{4}$ (b) $1\frac{1}{4} - \frac{1}{2}$ (c) $2\frac{3}{4} - 1\frac{1}{2}$ (d) $3\frac{1}{4} - 1\frac{1}{2}$ (e) $3 - 1\frac{3}{4}$

7 Kim ordered 2 Mega, 3 Maxi and 4 Mini colas.
What total volume of cola did she order?

Flour 3 kg   **Rice** 5 kg   **Beans** 2 kg   **Milk** 2·7l **Cream** 1·4l **Fruit Juice** 3·1l

1 Find each weight in grams and each volume in millilitres.

(a) $\frac{1}{5}$ of the flour   (b) $\frac{1}{10}$ of the rice   (c) $\frac{1}{4}$ of the beans

(d) $\frac{1}{2}$ of the cream   (e) $\frac{1}{9}$ of the milk   (f) $\frac{1}{100}$ of the fruit juice

2 (a) $\frac{1}{6}$ of £12·36   (b) $\frac{1}{3}$ of £15·45   (c) $\frac{1}{15}$ of £45·60   (d) $\frac{1}{1000}$ of £48 000

(e) $\frac{1}{9}$ of 3 hours   (f) $\frac{1}{20}$ of 4 hours   (g) $\frac{1}{40}$ of 6 hours   (h) $\frac{1}{12}$ of 2 hours

3 How many of each type of fruit were sold in the Tuck Shop during Healthy Eating Week?

	Number	Fraction sold
Apples	240	seven eighths
Melons	90	four fifths
Kiwis	120	five sixths
Oranges	110	seven tenths

4 (a) $\frac{3}{10}$ of 160   (b) $\frac{7}{100}$ of 2400   (c) $\frac{21}{1000}$ of 9000   (d) $\frac{7}{10}$ of 220

(e) $\frac{33}{100}$ of 800   (f) $\frac{63}{1000}$ of 3000   (g) $\frac{9}{10}$ of 110   (h) $\frac{47}{100}$ of 200

5 (a) $\frac{3}{4}$ of 600   (b) $\frac{5}{9}$ of 270   (c) $\frac{2}{7}$ of 420   (d) $\frac{5}{8}$ of 648

(e) $\frac{3}{5}$ of 405   (f) $\frac{4}{7}$ of 637   (g) $\frac{17}{20}$ of 2000   (h) $\frac{23}{40}$ of 1200

(i) $\frac{7}{8}$ of 4 m   (j) $\frac{3}{10}$ of £5   (k) $\frac{61}{100}$ of 2l (l) $\frac{27}{1000}$ of 3 kg

6 What fraction is   (a) 17p of £1   (b) 67 cm of 1 m   (c) 970 ml of 1l
(d) 350 g of 1 kg   (e) 450 m of 1 km   (f) 323 ml of 1l (g) 7p of £10?

7  The 2·8l of fruit punch is $\frac{2}{7}$ apple juice and $\frac{5}{8}$ peach juice.
The rest is orange juice.
What is the volume of the orange juice in millilitres?

1 Each of these children painted one fifth of the school mural. What total fraction of the mural did they paint?

2 Each of these children planted one eighth of the bulbs in the school garden. What fraction altogether of the bulbs did they plant?

3 (a) $7 \times \frac{1}{10}$　(b) $6 \times \frac{1}{7}$　(c) $2 \times \frac{1}{3}$　(d) $3 \times \frac{1}{4}$　(e) $5 \times \frac{1}{9}$

4 Each tin contains $\frac{1}{4}\ell$ of paint.

Find the total volume of paint in the tins.

5 (a) $6 \times \frac{1}{2}$　(b) $9 \times \frac{1}{3}$　(c) $10 \times \frac{1}{5}$　(d) $\frac{1}{6} \times 12$　(e) $15 \times \frac{1}{3}$

　(f) $20 \times \frac{1}{4}$　(g) $\frac{1}{2} \times 30$　(h) $40 \times \frac{1}{8}$　(i) $50 \times \frac{1}{10}$　(j) $80 \times \frac{1}{8}$

6 Each bag contains $\frac{1}{2}$ kg of bulbs.

Find the total weight of the bulbs.

7 (a) $7 \times \frac{2}{3}$　(b) $8 \times \frac{3}{5}$　(c) $\frac{3}{7} \times 6$　(d) $15 \times \frac{3}{8}$　(e) $22 \times \frac{2}{5}$

　(f) $\frac{7}{10} \times 5$　(g) $6 \times \frac{5}{8}$　(h) $8 \times \frac{5}{6}$　(i) $\frac{3}{10} \times 32$　(j) $6 \times \frac{5}{16}$

8 Three quarters of a litre of paint was used to paint each section of the school mural. How many litres of paint were used for
(a) 3 sections　(b) 5 sections
(c) 9 sections　(d) 10 sections?

1 At the Children's Farm there is 1 goose for every 3 hens.
There are 5 geese. How many hens are there?

2 The farm has 1 horse for every 4 dogs.
There are 12 dogs. How many horses are there?

3 There are 8 hens for every turkey.
There are 6 turkeys. How many hens are there?

4 Rachael feeds some animals turnips and carrots.
Find the missing numbers in the table.

Animal	Ratio of turnips to carrots	Number of turnips	Number of carrots
Horse	1 turnip to 3 carrots	6	**(a)**
Goat	3 turnips to 1 carrot	**(b)**	5
Donkey	2 turnips to 3 carrots	6	**(c)**
Sheep	3 turnips to 5 carrots	**(d)**	10

5 Rachael notices that there are 3 brown eggs for every 2 white eggs.
Find the number of white eggs when the number of brown eggs is

(a) 15   **(b)** 30   **(c)** 24   **(d)** 63.

1 At the farm, 2 rabbits in every 3 are long-haired.
There are 12 rabbits altogether.
How many are **(a)** long-haired **(b)** not long-haired?

2 4 in every 7 goats are male. There are 14 goats altogether.
How many are **(a)** male **(b)** female?

3 Rachael gives a total of 24 kilograms of feed to the goats and sheep
She gives the sheep 1 kg in every 4 kg of feed.
What weight of feed is given to **(a)** the sheep **(b)** the goats?

4 Alexander mixes 1 tin of white paint with
4 tins of green paint. He needs a total of
  ● 15 tins of paint for the stables
  ● 20 tins of paint for the barn.
How many tins of green paint does he need for
(a) the stables **(b)** the barn?

5 The table shows the numbers of larger
animals at the farm last year.
In **simplest form**, what was the ratio of

(a) horses to pigs
(b) sheep to cows
(c) horses to goats
(d) cows to pigs
(e) horses to animals
(f) pigs to animals?

Hillburn Children's Farm Numbers of larger animals	
Horses	6
Sheep	16
Goats	18
Pigs	12
Cows	8
	60

SPRING BULB CORNER

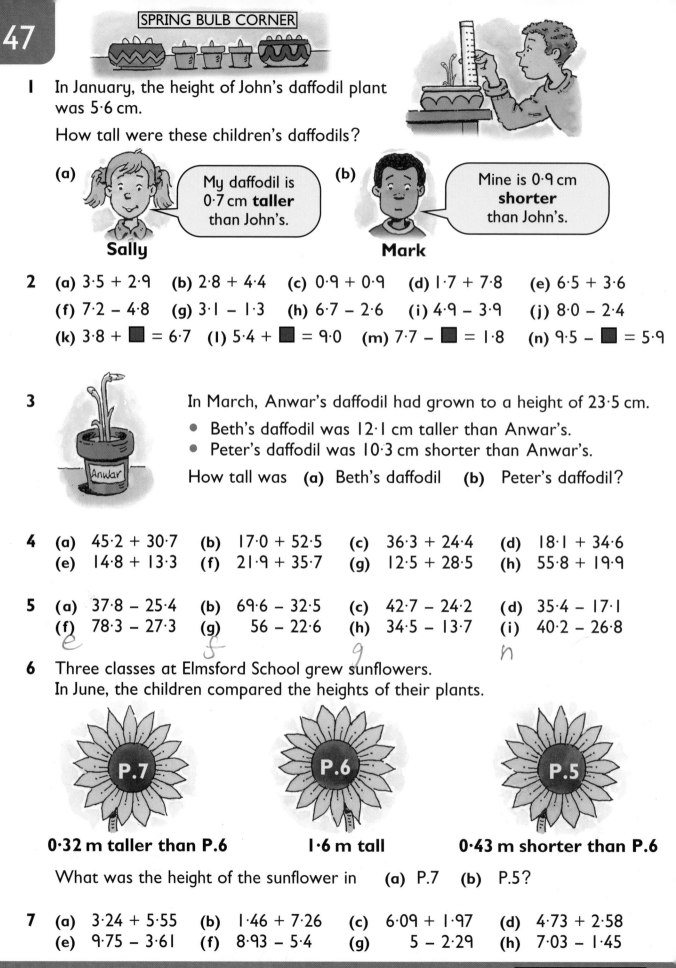

1 In January, the height of John's daffodil plant was 5·6 cm.

How tall were these children's daffodils?

(a) My daffodil is 0·7 cm **taller** than John's.

Sally

(b) Mine is 0·9 cm **shorter** than John's.

Mark

2 (a) 3·5 + 2·9   (b) 2·8 + 4·4   (c) 0·9 + 0·9   (d) 1·7 + 7·8   (e) 6·5 + 3·6

(f) 7·2 – 4·8   (g) 3·1 – 1·3   (h) 6·7 – 2·6   (i) 4·9 – 3·9   (j) 8·0 – 2·4

(k) 3·8 + ■ = 6·7   (l) 5·4 + ■ = 9·0   (m) 7·7 – ■ = 1·8   (n) 9·5 – ■ = 5·9

3 In March, Anwar's daffodil had grown to a height of 23·5 cm.

- Beth's daffodil was 12·1 cm taller than Anwar's.
- Peter's daffodil was 10·3 cm shorter than Anwar's.

How tall was   (a) Beth's daffodil   (b) Peter's daffodil?

4 (a) 45·2 + 30·7   (b) 17·0 + 52·5   (c) 36·3 + 24·4   (d) 18·1 + 34·6
(e) 14·8 + 13·3   (f) 21·9 + 35·7   (g) 12·5 + 28·5   (h) 55·8 + 19·9

5 (a) 37·8 – 25·4   (b) 69·6 – 32·5   (c) 42·7 – 24·2   (d) 35·4 – 17·1
(f) 78·3 – 27·3   (g)   56 – 22·6   (h) 34·5 – 13·7   (i) 40·2 – 26·8

6 Three classes at Elmsford School grew sunflowers.
In June, the children compared the heights of their plants.

P.7   P.6   P.5

0·32 m taller than P.6   1·6 m tall   0·43 m shorter than P.6

What was the height of the sunflower in   (a) P.7   (b) P.5?

7 (a) 3·24 + 5·55   (b) 1·46 + 7·26   (c) 6·09 + 1·97   (d) 4·73 + 2·58
(e) 9·75 – 3·61   (f) 8·93 – 5·4   (g)   5 – 2·29   (h) 7·03 – 1·45

1 Write the length of each jump **to the nearest tenth of 1 metre.**

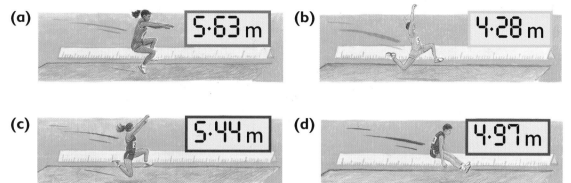

(a) 5·63 m

(b) 4·28 m

(c) 5·44 m

(d) 4·97 m

2 Write the height cleared by each pole-vaulter **to the nearest tenth of 1 metre.**

Gio	Franco	Bert	Danny
3·67 m	4·15 m	3·51 m	4·03 m

3 The table shows the results in the javelin competition.
Round each distance thrown **to the nearest whole metre.**

	Throw 1	Throw 2	Throw 3
Ellie	61·26 m	56·84 m	67·07 m
Cara	72·59 m	75·13 m	70·5 m
Alana	63·81 m	74·56 m	68·02 m

4 For each competitor, find

(a) the **approximate** total distance of Throws 1 and 2
(b) the approximate difference between Throws 1 and 2.

	Throw 1	Throw 2
Harry	16·41 m	18·3 m
Imo	12·26 m	19·85 m

5 Repeat question **4,** this time finding the **exact** totals and differences.

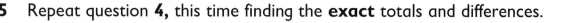

DIVING COMPETITION
Points awarded

Team	Semi-final	Final
China	243·1	254·7
Russia	240·8	245·5
USA	238·9	252·4
Australia	246·7	239·8
Japan	218·9	237·3
France	197·8	206·2

1   What was the total number of points awarded to each team for the semi-final and final?

2   What was the difference between the number of points awarded to each team for the semi-final and final?

SWIMMING RELAY FINALS
Times taken, in seconds, by winning teams to complete each 'leg'.

	Men's final	Women's final
1st leg	50·01	56·34
2nd leg	49·20	57·72
3rd leg	50·18	56·47
4th leg	48·69	55·55

3   Find, for each relay final, how many seconds altogether were taken to complete
   (a) the 1st and 2nd legs
   (b) the 2nd and 3rd legs
   (c) the 3rd and 4th legs
   (d) all 4 legs.

4   Find the difference, in seconds, between the times taken **for each leg** by male and female swimmers.

5   **(a)** 76·39 + 48·82   **(b)** 93·17 + 19·85   **(c)** 163·72 + 341·44
   (d) 98·76 – 55·18   **(e)** 47·29 – 23·82   **(f)** 72·58 – 16·41
   (g) 59·15 – 32·36   **(h)** 83·64 – 25·37   **(i)** 66·01 – 18·22
   (j) 80·07 – 29·68   **(k)** 90   – 42·63   **(l)** 267·58 – 104·79

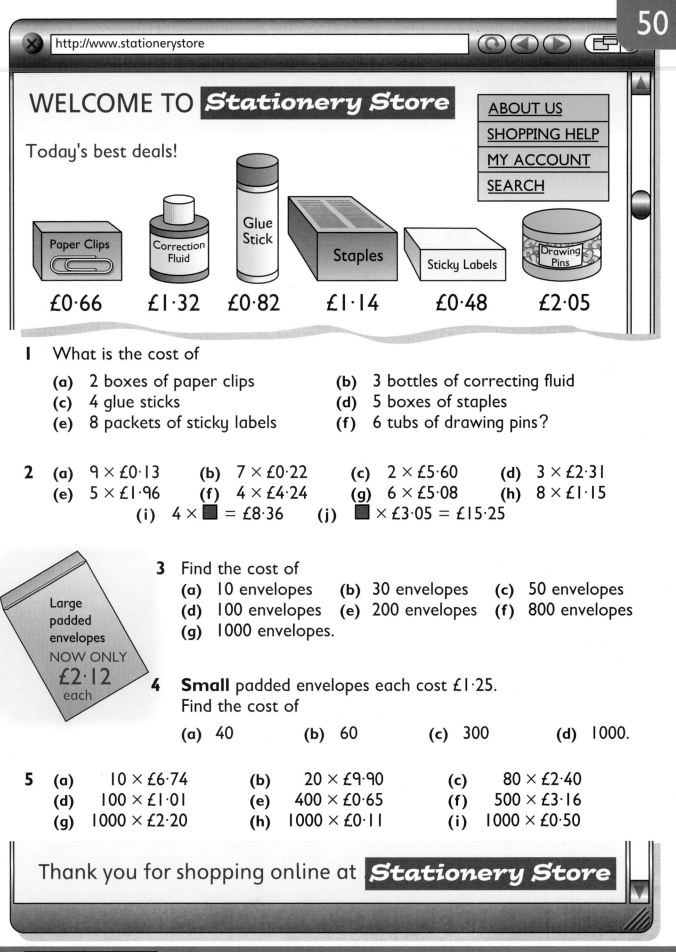

http://www.stationerystore

WELCOME TO *Stationery Store*

ABOUT US
SHOPPING HELP
MY ACCOUNT
SEARCH

Today's best deals!

Paper Clips	Correction Fluid	Glue Stick	Staples	Sticky Labels	Drawing Pins
£0·66	£1·32	£0·82	£1·14	£0·48	£2·05

1 What is the cost of

(a) 2 boxes of paper clips   (b) 3 bottles of correcting fluid
(c) 4 glue sticks   (d) 5 boxes of staples
(e) 8 packets of sticky labels   (f) 6 tubs of drawing pins?

2 (a) $9 \times £0·13$ (b) $7 \times £0·22$ (c) $2 \times £5·60$ (d) $3 \times £2·31$
(e) $5 \times £1·96$ (f) $4 \times £4·24$ (g) $6 \times £5·08$ (h) $8 \times £1·15$
(i) $4 \times \blacksquare = £8·36$ (j) $\blacksquare \times £3·05 = £15·25$

3 Find the cost of
(a) 10 envelopes   (b) 30 envelopes   (c) 50 envelopes
(d) 100 envelopes   (e) 200 envelopes   (f) 800 envelopes
(g) 1000 envelopes.

Large padded envelopes
NOW ONLY
£2·12
each

4 **Small** padded envelopes each cost £1·25.
Find the cost of

(a) 40   (b) 60   (c) 300   (d) 1000.

5 (a) $10 \times £6·74$ (b) $20 \times £9·90$ (c) $80 \times £2·40$
(d) $100 \times £1·01$ (e) $400 \times £0·65$ (f) $500 \times £3·16$
(g) $1000 \times £2·20$ (h) $1000 \times £0·11$ (i) $1000 \times £0·50$

Thank you for shopping online at *Stationery Store*

1 Children travel from their homes to Glenview School in different ways.

Mark walks

Jenna cycles

a **daily** return distance of 10·7 km.

a **daily** return distance of 14·2 km.

How many km does each child travel in
(a) 3 days (b) 5 days (c) 7 days?

2 (a) 2 × 34·5 (b) 4 × 12·6 (c) 20·8 × 3 (d) 9 × 10·4 (e) 11·3 × 8
(f) 6 × 13·9 (g) 14·7 × 5 (h) 2 × 53·1 (i) 4 × 31·6 (j) 48·5 × 3

3 Some children travel greater distances to the school.

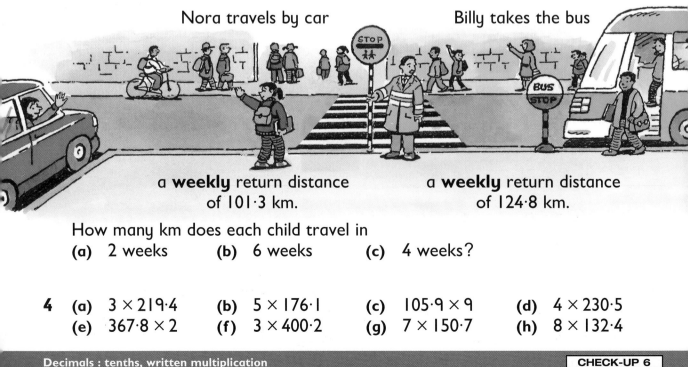

Nora travels by car

Billy takes the bus

a **weekly** return distance of 101·3 km.

a **weekly** return distance of 124·8 km.

How many km does each child travel in
(a) 2 weeks (b) 6 weeks (c) 4 weeks?

4 (a) 3 × 219·4 (b) 5 × 176·1 (c) 105·9 × 9 (d) 4 × 230·5
(e) 367·8 × 2 (f) 3 × 400·2 (g) 7 × 150·7 (h) 8 × 132·4

1 *Sound City* sells loudspeaker cable in metre lengths.

Finetune		£1·32 per m
Senso		£0·85 per m
Puresound		£2·16 per m
Bassflex		£5·79 per m
Corewire		£3·08 per m
Truebeat		£4·60 per m

How much would each of these lengths of cable cost?

(a) 3 m of *Finetune* (b) 4 m of *Senso* (c) 6 m of *Puresound*

(d) 5 m of *Bassflex* (e) 9 m of *Corewire* (f) 7 m of *Truebeat*

2 (a) $3 \times 6·12$ (b) $2 \times 5·47$ (c) $8 \times 3·18$ (d) $4 \times 2·69$

  (e) $5 \times 4·84$ (f) $6 \times 8·75$ (g) $7 \times 7·77$ (h) $9 \times 9·09$

3

Amplifier:
6 monthly payments of £31·05

System: 9 monthly payments of £60·21

What is the total cost, using monthly payments, of

(a) the amplifier (b) the system?

4 (a) $2 \times 34·12$ (b) $3 \times 20·31$ (c) $4 \times 22·06$ (d) $5 \times 11·71$

  (e) $6 \times 10·45$ (f) $2 \times 43·98$ (g) $7 \times 14·63$ (h) $8 \times 12·54$

  (i) $9 \times 25·36$ (j) $5 \times 37·29$ (k) $8 \times 48·57$ (l) $7 \times 70·07$

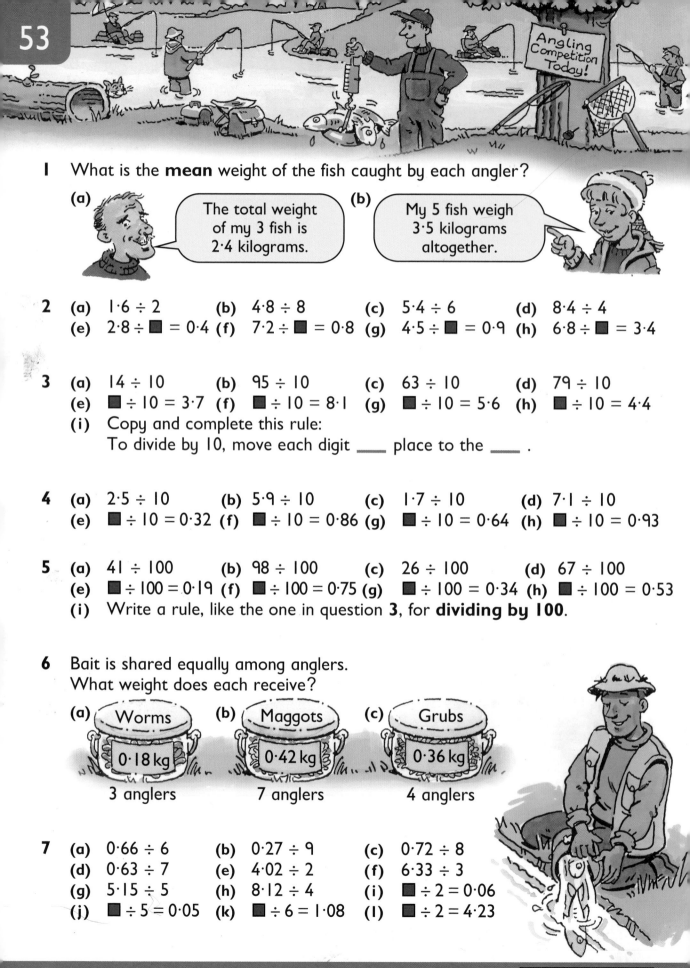

53

1 What is the **mean** weight of the fish caught by each angler?

(a) The total weight of my 3 fish is 2·4 kilograms.

(b) My 5 fish weigh 3·5 kilograms altogether.

2 (a) $1·6 \div 2$ (b) $4·8 \div 8$ (c) $5·4 \div 6$ (d) $8·4 \div 4$
   (e) $2·8 \div \blacksquare = 0·4$ (f) $7·2 \div \blacksquare = 0·8$ (g) $4·5 \div \blacksquare = 0·9$ (h) $6·8 \div \blacksquare = 3·4$

3 (a) $14 \div 10$ (b) $95 \div 10$ (c) $63 \div 10$ (d) $79 \div 10$
   (e) $\blacksquare \div 10 = 3·7$ (f) $\blacksquare \div 10 = 8·1$ (g) $\blacksquare \div 10 = 5·6$ (h) $\blacksquare \div 10 = 4·4$
   (i) Copy and complete this rule:
     To divide by 10, move each digit ____ place to the ____ .

4 (a) $2·5 \div 10$ (b) $5·9 \div 10$ (c) $1·7 \div 10$ (d) $7·1 \div 10$
   (e) $\blacksquare \div 10 = 0·32$ (f) $\blacksquare \div 10 = 0·86$ (g) $\blacksquare \div 10 = 0·64$ (h) $\blacksquare \div 10 = 0·93$

5 (a) $41 \div 100$ (b) $98 \div 100$ (c) $26 \div 100$ (d) $67 \div 100$
   (e) $\blacksquare \div 100 = 0·19$ (f) $\blacksquare \div 100 = 0·75$ (g) $\blacksquare \div 100 = 0·34$ (h) $\blacksquare \div 100 = 0·53$
   (i) Write a rule, like the one in question **3**, for **dividing by 100**.

6 Bait is shared equally among anglers.
What weight does each receive?

(a) Worms   0·18 kg   3 anglers

(b) Maggots   0·42 kg   7 anglers

(c) Grubs   0·36 kg   4 anglers

7 (a) $0·66 \div 6$ (b) $0·27 \div 9$ (c) $0·72 \div 8$
   (d) $0·63 \div 7$ (e) $4·02 \div 2$ (f) $6·33 \div 3$
   (g) $5·15 \div 5$ (h) $8·12 \div 4$ (i) $\blacksquare \div 2 = 0·06$
   (j) $\blacksquare \div 5 = 0·05$ (k) $\blacksquare \div 6 = 1·08$ (l) $\blacksquare \div 2 = 4·23$

Cities Direct - Fares from Glasgow

Tickets	To Edinburgh		To Inverness	
	Adult	Child	Adult	Child
Single	£4·95	£3·15	£11·85	£8·05
Return	£7·99	£5·20	£19·25	£12·70
Day Saver	£6·10	£3·90	£14·12	£10·98

Work mentally, rounding all amounts to the nearest pound.

1 **Approximately** how much is collected in fares for these tickets on the coach to **Edinburgh**?

(a) 6 adult Singles (b) 4 child Singles (c) 8 adult Returns
(d) 3 child Returns (e) 7 adult and 7 child Day Savers

2 **Approximately** how much is collected in fares to **Inverness** for

(a) 2 adult Returns (b) 9 child Returns (c) 5 adult Day Savers
(d) 20 child Day Savers (e) 30 adult and 25 child Singles?

3 **Cities Direct - Daily Hire Charges**

Microbus	Minibus	Coach	Maxibus
£53·80	£96·30	£199·99	£350·28

What is the **approximate** cost **per passenger** of hiring for one day

● a Microbus for (a) 2 passengers (b) 3 passengers
● a Minibus for (c) 4 passengers (d) 6 passengers
● a Coach for (e) 20 passengers (f) 25 passengers
● a Maxibus for (g) 50 passengers (h) 70 passengers?

4 Find the **approximate** value of

(a) $(5 \times £14·92) + (9 \times £20·17)$ (b) $(£96·40 \div 8) - (£53·64 \div 6)$
(c) $(£12·11 \times 4) - (£179·73 \div 9)$ (d) $(£240·21 \div 3) + (8 \times £50·94)$.

5 Repeat question **4**, this time finding the **exact** values.

1 Rosie can cut a roll of cellophane, 10·8 m long, into sheets
to wrap **either** 9 small bouquets **or** 6 large bouquets.
On average, what length of cellophane does she use for

  (a) a small bouquet **(b)** a large bouquet?

2 **(a)** 25·2 ÷ 3 **(b)** 58·8 ÷ 6 **(c)** 22·8 ÷ 4 **(d)** 34·5 ÷ 5

3 Rosie uses a piece of ribbon,
91·5 cm long to tie 3 bouquets.
On average, what length of ribbon
does she use **per bouquet**?

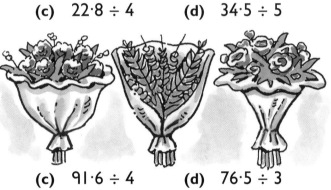

4 **(a)** 61·8 ÷ 2 **(b)** 92·7 ÷ 9 **(c)** 91·6 ÷ 4 **(d)** 76·5 ÷ 3

5 Some of Rosie's floral decorations include bows. Find the **mean** length of
ribbon used to make each type of bow.

  (a) **Shoestring** **(b)** **Puffy** **(c)** **Florist's**

120·8 m of ribbon   102·6 m of ribbon   101·5 m of ribbon
for 8 bows   for 9 bows   for 7 bows

6 **(a)** 348·4 ÷ 4 **(b)** 672·7 ÷ 7 **(c)** 231·5 ÷ 5 **(d)** 458·4 ÷ 8

7 **(a)** 954·9 ÷ 9 **(b)** 552·9 ÷ 3 **(c)** 285·6 ÷ 2 **(d)** 967·2 ÷ 8
  (e) 803·6 ÷ 7 **(f)** 737·2 ÷ 4 **(g)** 623·5 ÷ 5 **(h)** 791·4 ÷ 6

1 A **box** of daffodils costs *Flowers 4U* £4·95. What is the cost **per bunch** when Rosie splits the daffodils into

    (a) 5 bunches   **(b)** 9 bunches?

2 **(a)** £1·24 ÷ 4   **(b)** £1·62 ÷ 2   **(c)** £5·18 ÷ 7   **(d)** £4·98 ÷ 6

3 A box of carnations costs *Flowers 4U* £8·64. What is the cost per bunch when Rosie splits the carnations into

    (a) 8 bunches   **(b)** 3 bunches?

4 **(a)** £5·38 ÷ 2   **(b)** £7·85 ÷ 5   **(c)** £9·04 ÷ 4   **(d)** £9·73 ÷ 7

5

Flowers 4U charges £30·24 to supply a restaurant with 7 vases of flowers. On average, what is the charge **per vase**?

6 **(a)** £24·54 ÷ 6 **(b)** £64·98 ÷ 9
    (c) £26·01 ÷ 3 **(d)** £57·36 ÷ 8

7 Rosie delivers flowers to 4 customers and charges £84·96 altogether. How much does each customer pay, on average, for their flowers?

8 **(a)** £69·36 ÷ 3   **(b)** £65·46 ÷ 6
    (c) £48·54 ÷ 2   **(d)** £81·05 ÷ 5
    (e) £94·14 ÷ 9   **(f)** £72·66 ÷ 7
    (g) £37·50 ÷ 2   **(h)** £95·92 ÷ 8

1 **(a)** Find the cost of 8 single tins.

(b) Does the multipack give better value for money? Explain.

£1·31   multipack £9·92

2 **(a)** How much does **one** tin of beans cost in
- the family pack
- the economy pack?

(b) Which pack gives better value? Explain.

family pack   economy pack
£2·58   £4·14

3 Which pack gives better value? Explain each time.

(a)

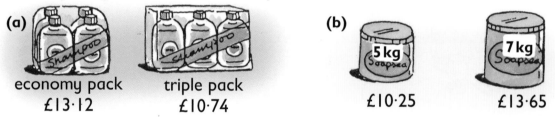

economy pack   triple pack
£13·12   £10·74

(b)

5 kg Soapsea   7 kg Soapsea

£10·25   £13·65

4 Dave makes up multipacks for *Price Co*. He decides their prices by taking one sixth off each **total** cost of buying several single items. What price would Dave make each of these multipacks?

(a)

single box costs £1·53

(b)

single packet costs £1·26

(c)

single bottle costs £3·16

5 What is the cost of

(a) 5 cans   **(b)** 1 can

(c) 4 boxes   **(d)** 1 box?

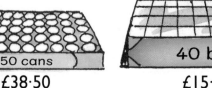

50 cans
£38·50

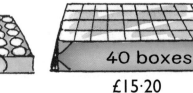

40 boxes
£15·20

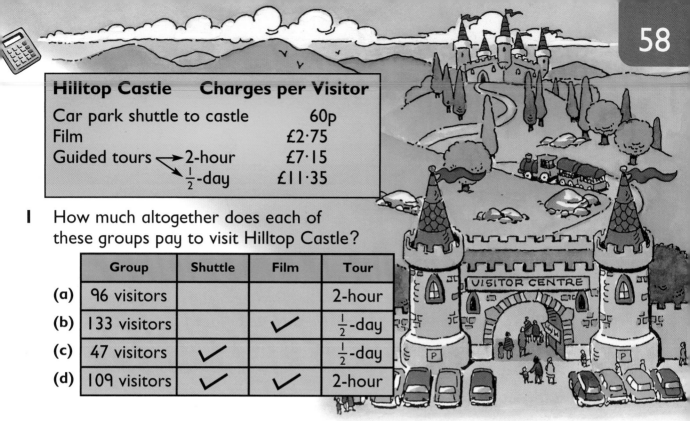

Hilltop Castle	Charges per Visitor
Car park shuttle to castle	60p
Film	£2·75
Guided tours → 2-hour	£7·15
½-day	£11·35

1 How much altogether does each of these groups pay to visit Hilltop Castle?

	Group	Shuttle	Film	Tour
(a)	96 visitors			2-hour
(b)	133 visitors		✓	½-day
(c)	47 visitors	✓		½-day
(d)	109 visitors	✓	✓	2-hour

2 A touring party of 62 visitors pays a special total price of £820·26 to use the shuttle, watch the film and take the ½-day tour.
How much is the saving on the normal price **(a)** altogether **(b)** per visitor?

3 On each trip to the castle a shuttle can carry 24 passengers.
When there are 174 visitors:

(a) how many shuttle trips are **needed**
(b) how many shuttles are **full**
(c) how many passengers are on the shuttle which is **not** full?

4 The film theatre has 19 seats in each row.
When there are 446 visitors:

(a) how many rows are needed
(b) how many rows are full
(c) how many people are in the row which is not full?

5 There are 33 audio guide headphones in each box. When there are 289 visitors:

(a) how many boxes must be opened
(b) how many whole boxes are used
(c) how many headphones are taken from the box which is not completely used?

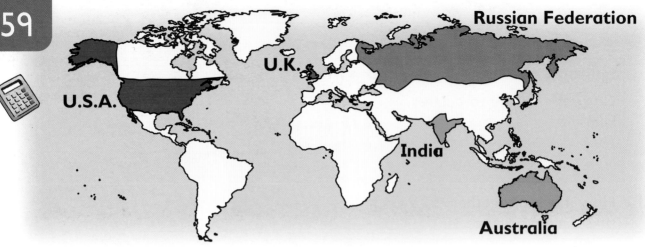

Round each answer to the nearest whole number.

1 The United Kingdom has an area of about 244 082 square kilometres (km²).
About how many times greater than the U.K. is the area of

  (a) U.S.A. - 9 809 386 km²   **(b)** Russian Federation - 17 075 400 km²
  (c) India - 3 287 263 km²   **(d)** Australia - 7 688 700 km²?

2 Scotland has an area of about 78 772 km².
About how many times greater is the area
of each of these American States?

  (a) California - 423 999 km²
  (b) Texas - 695 673 km²
  (c) Florida - 170 312 km²

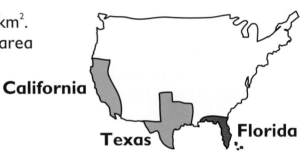

3 The average number of people who live within 1 km² of land is called
the **population density**.
The population density of The Netherlands is **about 372 people per km²,**
the highest in the World.

Find, in people per km², the approximate population density of

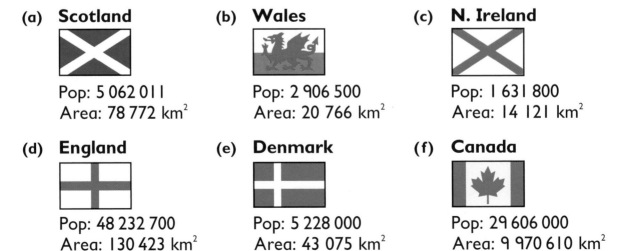

(a) Scotland
Pop: 5 062 011
Area: 78 772 km²

(b) Wales
Pop: 2 906 500
Area: 20 766 km²

(c) N. Ireland
Pop: 1 631 800
Area: 14 121 km²

(d) England
Pop: 48 232 700
Area: 130 423 km²

(e) Denmark
Pop: 5 228 000
Area: 43 075 km²

(f) Canada
Pop: 29 606 000
Area: 9 970 610 km²

1 Anna's baggage weighs **8·247 kg** or **8$\frac{247}{1000}$ kg** or **8247 thousandths of 1 kg**.

Write each of these weights in other ways.

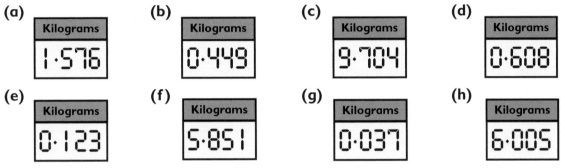

(a) Kilograms 1·576

(b) Kilograms 0·449

(c) Kilograms 9·704

(d) Kilograms 0·608

(e) Kilograms 0·123

(f) Kilograms 5·851

(g) Kilograms 0·037

(h) Kilograms 6·005

2 Write each weight in decimal form.

(a) $\frac{982}{1000}$ kg **(b)** $\frac{566}{1000}$ kg **(c)** $\frac{17}{1000}$ kg **(d)** 309 thousandths of 1 kg

(e) 2$\frac{294}{1000}$ kg **(f)** 7$\frac{473}{1000}$ kg **(g)** 4$\frac{5}{1000}$ kg **(h)** 8708 thousandths of 1 kg

3 Copy and complete each sequence.

(a) 0·347, 0·348, 0·349, ___, ___, ___, 0·353

(b) 1·094, 1·096, 1·098, ___, ___, ___, 1·106

(c) 0·716, 0·712, 0·708, ___, ___, ___, 0·692

(d) 3·515, 3·510, 3·505, ___, ___, ___, 3·485

(e) 0·283, 0·483, 0·683, ___, ___, ___, 1·483

(f) 4·199, 4·298, 4·397, ___, ___, ___, 4·793

4 Write the 3-place decimal fraction between

(a) 0·124 and 0·126 **(b)** 3·817 and 3·819
(c) 6·305 and 6·307 **(d)** 5·032 and 5·034

5 Write a 3-place decimal fraction between

(a) 0·997 and 1·002 **(b)** 1·231 and 1·321
(c) 9·589 and 9·6 **(d)** 4·45 and 4·46

1 What is the value of the purple digit in each display?

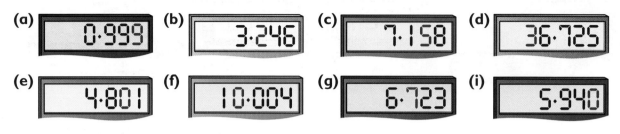

(a) 0·999   (b) 3·246   (c) 7·158   (d) 36·725

(e) 4·801   (f) 10·004   (g) 6·723   (i) 5·940

2 Which number on the cards has

(a) 8 thousandths   (b) 6 tenths
(c) 7 hundredths   (d) 4 tens
(e) the largest thousandths digit
(f) the smallest thousandths digit
(g) a thousandths digit half of the
    tenths digit?

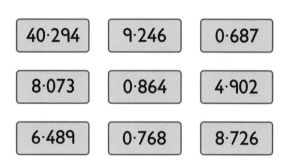

40·294	9·246	0·687
8·073	0·864	4·902
6·489	0·768	8·726

3 Write each number as a 3-place decimal fraction.

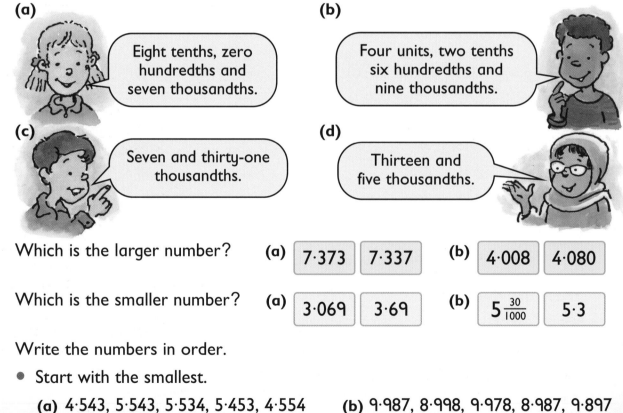

(a) Eight tenths, zero hundredths and seven thousandths.

(b) Four units, two tenths six hundredths and nine thousandths.

(c) Seven and thirty-one thousandths.

(d) Thirteen and five thousandths.

4 Which is the larger number? (a) 7·373   7·337   (b) 4·008   4·080

5 Which is the smaller number? (a) 3·069   3·69   (b) $5\frac{30}{1000}$ 5·3

6 Write the numbers in order.

• Start with the smallest.

(a) 4·543, 5·543, 5·534, 5·453, 4·554   (b) 9·987, 8·998, 9·978, 8·987, 9·897

• Start with the largest.

(c) 2·201, 2·102, 1·21, 2·212, 1·212   (d) 6·5, 7·556, 6·765, 7·5, 7·65

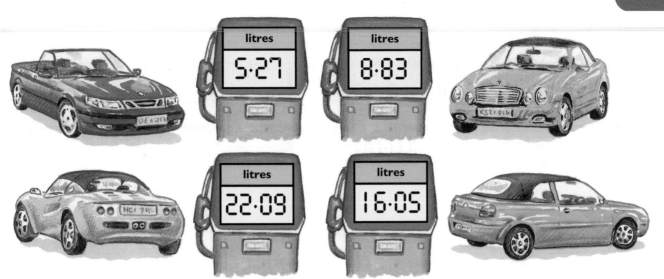

1   Write the reading on each fuel pump **to the nearest tenth of 1 litre.**

2   Write each of these volumes to the nearest tenth of 1 litre.

(a) litres	(b) litres	(c) litres	(d) litres
0·416	3·782	14·055	37·006

3

	Lap 1	Lap 2
	41·2 s	37·5 s
	48·91 s	43·67 s
	39·497 s	39·501 s
	52·086 s	54·742 s

The table shows the **practice** lap times, in seconds, for each car.

List the lap times for each rounded to the nearest **whole number** of seconds.

4   These are the cars' **race** times in seconds.

Lap 1	40·7 s	47·09 s	36·168 s	53·004 s
Lap 2	36·2 s	41·83 s	29·522 s	59·519 s

For each car, round the race times to the nearest whole number of seconds then find
(a)   its **approximate** total time for Lap 1 and Lap 2
(b)   the **approximate** difference between its times for Lap 1 and Lap 2.

5   Find the **exact** totals and differences in questions **4 (a)** and **4 (b).**

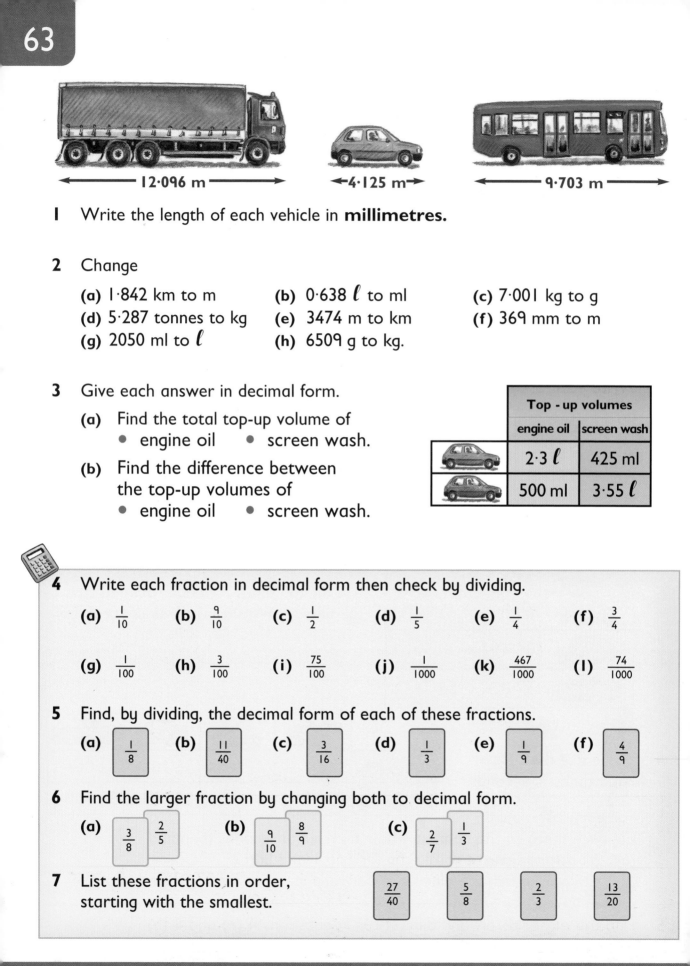

←——— 12·096 m ———→ ←4·125 m→ ←——— 9·703 m ———→

1 Write the length of each vehicle in **millimetres.**

2 Change

(a) 1·842 km to m   (b) 0·638 ℓ to ml   (c) 7·001 kg to g
(d) 5·287 tonnes to kg   (e) 3474 m to km   (f) 369 mm to m
(g) 2050 ml to ℓ (h) 6509 g to kg.

3 Give each answer in decimal form.

(a) Find the total top-up volume of
  • engine oil   • screen wash.

(b) Find the difference between
  the top-up volumes of
  • engine oil   • screen wash.

Top - up volumes		
	engine oil	screen wash
	2·3 ℓ	425 ml
	500 ml	3·55 ℓ

4 Write each fraction in decimal form then check by dividing.

(a) $\frac{1}{10}$ (b) $\frac{9}{10}$ (c) $\frac{1}{2}$ (d) $\frac{1}{5}$ (e) $\frac{1}{4}$ (f) $\frac{3}{4}$

(g) $\frac{1}{100}$ (h) $\frac{3}{100}$ (i) $\frac{75}{100}$ (j) $\frac{1}{1000}$ (k) $\frac{467}{1000}$ (l) $\frac{74}{1000}$

5 Find, by dividing, the decimal form of each of these fractions.

(a) $\frac{1}{8}$ (b) $\frac{11}{40}$ (c) $\frac{3}{16}$ (d) $\frac{1}{3}$ (e) $\frac{1}{9}$ (f) $\frac{4}{9}$

6 Find the larger fraction by changing both to decimal form.

(a) $\frac{3}{8}$ $\frac{2}{5}$ (b) $\frac{9}{10}$ $\frac{8}{9}$ (c) $\frac{2}{7}$ $\frac{1}{3}$

7 List these fractions in order,
starting with the smallest. $\frac{27}{40}$ $\frac{5}{8}$ $\frac{2}{3}$ $\frac{13}{20}$

1 Write as a fraction **and** as a percentage.

(a) 31 out of 100   (b) 30 out of 60   (c) 20 out of 200

(d) 100 out of 500   (e) 7 out of 100   (f) 50 out of 1000

2 Find the **percentage**

(a) **not** cotton   (b) **not** wool   (c) **not** nylon.

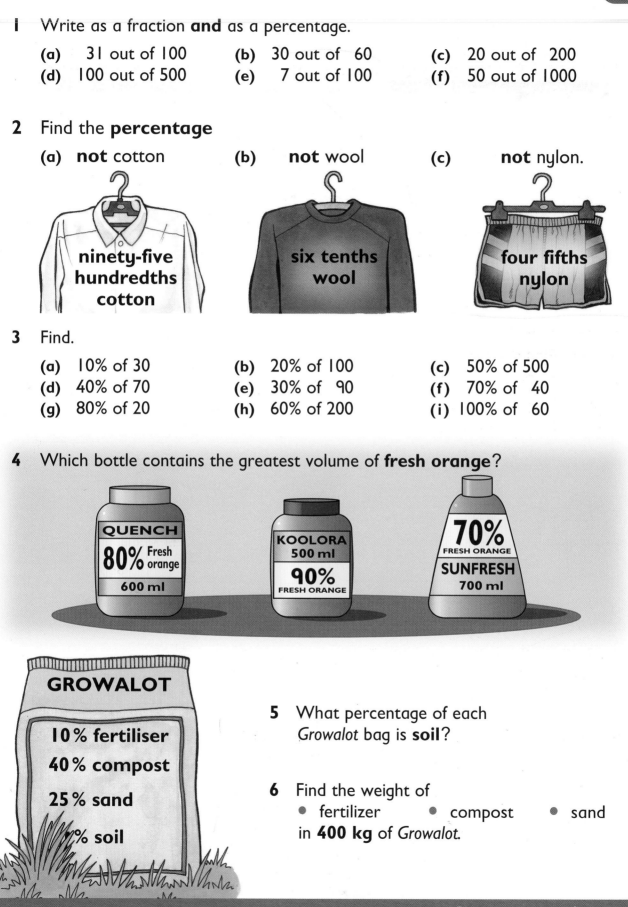

ninety-five hundredths cotton

six tenths wool

four fifths nylon

3 Find.

(a) 10% of 30   (b) 20% of 100   (c) 50% of 500

(d) 40% of 70   (e) 30% of 90   (f) 70% of 40

(g) 80% of 20   (h) 60% of 200   (i) 100% of 60

4 Which bottle contains the greatest volume of **fresh orange**?

QUENCH
80% Fresh orange
600 ml

KOOLORA
500 ml
90%
FRESH ORANGE

70%
FRESH ORANGE
SUNFRESH
700 ml

GROWALOT

10% fertiliser

40% compost

25% sand

% soil

5 What percentage of each *Growalot* bag is **soil**?

6 Find the weight of
- fertilizer
- compost
- sand

in **400 kg** of *Growalot*.

1 Write as a percentage.

(a) 9 out of 90   (b) 7 out of 35   (c) 60 out of 80
(d) 15 out of 60   (e) 14 out of 70   (f) 23 out of 46
(g) 4 out of 10   (h) 1 out of 20   (i) 17 out of 50

2 (a) How many test questions did Kelly answer incorrectly?

10% of my 40 answers were wrong.

Kelly

(b) For what length of the race was Liam in the lead?

I led for 25% of the 1 kilometre race.

Liam

(c) How much money did Sunil spend?

I spent 25% of my £300 savings.

Sunil

(d) How much money did Gaby give to her sister?

I gave 30% of my £5 pocket money to my sister.

Gaby

(e) What length of Una's rope is frayed?

40% of this 3 metre rope is frayed.

Una

(f) How many of Adam's stamps are British?

75% of my 200 stamps are British.

Adam

(g) What weight of potatoes has Harry?

I have 5 kilograms of vegetables. 70% are potatoes.

Harry

(h) What volume of Lucy's punch is orange juice?

I made 30 litres of fruit punch. $33\frac{1}{3}$% is orange juice.

Lucy

3 Find

(a) 5% of 80   (b) 15% of 60   (c) 13% of 200
(d) $12\frac{1}{2}$% of 1600   (e) $2\frac{1}{2}$% of 120   (f) 11% of 1000.

1 Write as a percentage.

(a) 0·15   (b) $\frac{3}{10}$ (c) 0·91   (d) $\frac{7}{20}$ (e) 0·06   (f) $\frac{9}{50}$

2 Write in two other ways.

(a) 43%   (b) $\frac{8}{25}$ (c) 0·7   (d) $\frac{3}{5}$ (e) 8%   (f) 0·12

3 (a) Which of these numbers is equivalent to 65 %?

6·5	$6\frac{1}{5}$	0·65	65·0

(b) Which of these percentages is the equivalent to 0·27?

0·27%	2·7%	27%	270%

4 Which is greater

(a) 37% or $\frac{4}{10}$ (b) 0·8 or 75%   (c) 22 % or 2·2   (d) $\frac{1}{20}$ or 20 %?

5 Write True (T) or False (F).

(a) 30% < $\frac{2}{5}$ (b) 0·1 > 11%   (c) $\frac{40}{50}$ < 70 %   (d) 10 % > 0·01

6 Write the numbers which are

(a) greater than one half	$\frac{3}{4}$	38 %	$\frac{3}{8}$	0·6	55 %
(b) smaller than one quarter.	0·3	24 %	$\frac{4}{20}$	0·26	40 %

7 List in order, starting with the **smallest** number.

9   99   9%   0·9   99%

8 Copy and complete each sequence.

(a) 10%, 0·15, $\frac{20}{100}$, 25%, ___, ___, ___, 0·45, $\frac{50}{100}$

(b) $\frac{20}{100}$, 0·18, 16%, ___, 0·12, ___, ___, ___, 4%

1 A school group of fifty people
   is visiting the London Eye.
   ● 10% are adults
   ● 58% are girls
   How many are **boys**?

2 Bigcity United's ticket prices are about to
   rise by 5%.
   What will the new price of this ticket be?

3 Sixty fair-haired children are 30% of the total number who attend
   Brockley School.
   How many children altogether attend the school?

4 Bigcity United played
   thirty games last season.
   They won 60% of these.
   How many games did they **lose**?

5

   I had twenty-four
   out of thirty-two
   questions correct
   in a sports quiz.

   Jamie

   I was correct in
   one hundred and forty-
   eight questions out of
   two hundred in a pop
   music quiz.

   Roz

   Who had the greater **percentage** of questions correct?

6

Discount Vouchers

Half price
any item costing
less than £50

Take 10% off
any item

Take £6 off
any item

What is the **cheapest** total cost of the four items,
using the *Discount Vouchers*? Explain.

1 Calculate the number of each title sold by *e-books* from January to June.

e-books... Internet Bookshop...

Title	Number in Warehouse (January)	% sold by June
Wizard's Revenge	825	12%
Jokes Galore	550	2%
Money Matters	475	16%
Return to Sunway	350	14%
Good Food	125	8%
Fame for a Day	700	28%
Up and Away	750	26%

2 **(a)** 22% of 1650 **(b)** 4% of 6750 **(c)** 35% of 7020 **(d)** 24% of 7650
(e) 6% of 27 150 **(f)** 72% of 11 250 **(g)** 34% of 14 450 **(h)** 46% of 19 550

3 Find, **to the nearest whole number:**

(a) 11% of 840 **(b)** 20% of 654 **(c)** 36% of 690 **(d)** 25% of 430
(e) 13% of 658 **(f)** 27% of 459 **(g)** 5% of 909 **(h)** 61% of 782
(i) 17% of 2646 **(j)** 15% of 2135 **(k)** 7% of 2997 **(l)** 19% of 3425

4 How many copies of each title were sold from July to December?

e-books... Internet Bookshop...

Title	January - June Copies sold	July - December Copies sold - % change
Socceroo	1250	+56%
Scary Tales	2050	−18%
A Knight's Tale	1175	+32%
Dreams	1620	+45%
Magic Tricks	1050	−42%
World View	1240	+65%
Camping	2880	−55%
Pet Care	2125	−68%

1 Find each child's **two-digit** house number.

Rhona:
Mine is a **square** number.
Both of its digits are also
square numbers.

Robbie:
Mine is a **prime** number.
The product of its digits is less than 5.
The sum of its digits is divisible by 5.

2 Copy Robbie's triangle each time.
Place each number from 1 to 6 in a circle
so that the sum in each line equals

(a) 9 **(b)** 10 **(c)** 11 **(d)** 12.

3
I have only tiger barbs
and silver sharks in my tank.
There are 34 fish altogether.
There are 8 more tiger barbs
than silver sharks.

How many of each type of fish are in Rhona's tank?

4

0	15	8	1
14	11	6	9
5	10	12	7
3	13	4	2

Copy this 0 to 15 number grid on squared paper.
Divide the grid into 4 **identically shaped** pieces,
each with the same total.

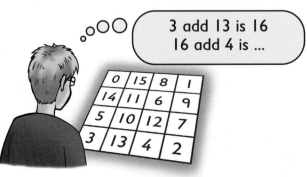

3 add 13 is 16
16 add 4 is ...

Week day Menu

Starters	Soup
	Juice
Main courses	Chicken
	Fish
	Pizza

I'll have the soup and the chicken please.

1 **(a)** List all the different meals consisting of a Starter and a Main course that a customer can order.

(b) Mario, the chef, adds Mussels to the Starters.
List all the **extra** meals that are now available.

2 **(a)** At the weekend, Mario adds Desserts to the menu.
List all the different meals consisting of three courses that a customer can order.

(b) List the **additional** three-course meals that can be ordered when Tagliatelle is added to the Main courses.

Weekend Menu

Starters	Soup
	Juice
	Mussels
Main courses	Chicken
	Fish
	Pizza
Desserts	Ice cream
	Gateau

3 Mario's pizzas each have three toppings. Customers can choose from Olives, Tomato, Pepperoni, Mushrooms and Tuna.

Make a list of all the different pizzas with three toppings that can be served.

1 In a badminton tournament each player plays one game against every other player.

2 players   **3 players**   **4 players**

1 game   3 games

(a) Draw a diagram to find the number of games when there are 4 players.

(b) Copy this table.

Number of players	2	3	4	5
Number of games	1	3		

How many games do you **think** there are for 5 players? Draw a diagram to check your answer.

(c) **Without drawing** diagrams, extend your table to show the number of games for 6, 7, 8, 9 and 10 players.

2 (a) Sid counts the number of poles used to make each row of pentagons.

1 pentagon   **2 pentagons**   **3 pentagons**

5 poles   9 poles   13 poles

Draw a row of 4 pentagons and find the number of poles.

(b) Make a table of results and extend it, without drawing, to show the number of poles in rows of up to 10 pentagons.

Number of pentagons	1	2	3
Number of poles	5	9	13

3 (a) Draw shapes to find the number of diagonals when the shape has
 • 3 sides   • 4 sides   • 5 sides   • 6 sides.

(b) How many diagonals do you **think** a shape with 7 sides has? Check by drawing.

(c) Without drawing shapes, make a table to show the number of diagonals in shapes with up to 10 sides.

I Bob, Ron, Joe and Alf are footballers.

Use these clues to match each player to his number and the position he plays.

- Joe is the *striker*
- The *goalie* is not standing next to the *striker*.
- The *winger* wears the largest number
- Alf and the *midfielder* are best friends.
- Joe's number is 19.
- Bob is standing between Alf and Joe.

2 A number whose digits read the same forwards and backwards is called a **palindromic number**.

22   20102   313   888   7447

(a) List all of the three-digit **palindromes** that begin with 5.

(b)  What will be the next palindromic number to show on this car's mileometer?

3 Explain what the numbers in each set have in common.

(a)

92	324	7209
282 613		200
	1 504 722	

(b)

20	365	95
1215		4 35 610
	7000	

(c)

25	85	14
96	47	63

(d)

91	2314	46
532	28	712

1 In one hexagon the perimeter = 6.

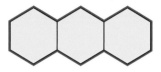 When two hexagons are joined, side-by-side, the perimeter = 10.

(a) What is the perimeter when

- three hexagons are joined
- four hexagons are joined?

(b) What is the perimeter when

- ten hexagons are joined
- fifteen hexagons are joined?

2 In an inter-school basketball tournament, three schools played each other home and away. In the six games:

- Ashton did not defeat Bigton
- Curdy did not lose a home game
- no games were drawn
- Curdy lost twice.

What was the result of each of the games?

3 During the badminton season:

- Ashton won three times as many games as Curdy
- Curdy won a quarter of the games won by Bigton
- Bigton won three more games than Ashon.

Which school won **twelve** games?

4

MURRAY'S MOTORS   GREAT NEW CAR DEAL!!

CHOOSE ANY COMBINATION OF 2 OPTIONS FREE!

Options available

- air conditioning
- heated seats
- metallic paint
- CD player
- alloy wheels
- spoiler

How many different 2-option packages can be chosen?

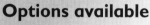

1 Write each weight in grams, to the nearest 10 g.

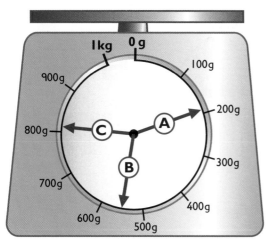
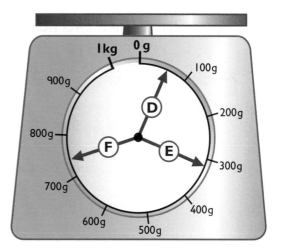

2 Write each weight in kilograms, to the nearest 0·01 kg.

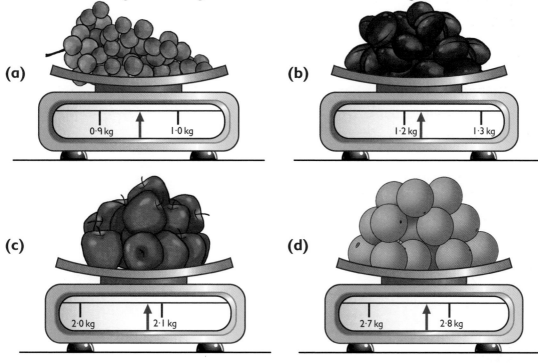

(a) 0·9 kg   1·0 kg

(b) 1·2 kg   1·3 kg

(c) 2·0 kg   2·1 kg

(d) 2·7 kg   2·8 kg

3 Find the weight of a bag of cubes
- in grams, to the nearest 10 g
- in kilograms, to the nearest 0·01 kg.

4 Make up a bag of sand weighing about 410 grams.

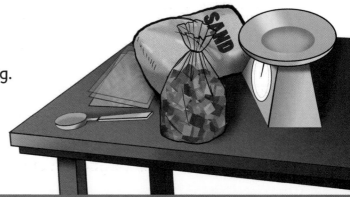

1 Write each weight in kilograms.

(a)

(b)

(c)

11 tonnes 950 kg　　　**34 tonnes 750 kg**　　　**4 tonnes 500 kg**

2 Write each weight in tonnes and kilograms.

(a)　　　　　　　　　(b)　　　　　　　　　(c)

5900 kg　　　　　　**3300 kg**　　　　　**13 050 kg**

3 A single-decker bus weighs about 8500 kg.
Fourteen adults have a total weight
of about 1 tonne.
There are 42 adults on the bus.
What is the approximate total
weight of the bus and the
people in kilograms?

4

Sleepers 90 kg each　Slabs 20 kg each　Gravel 500 kg bag

An unloaded truck weighs 5 tonnes.
When it leaves the depot it is
transporting:

- 4 bags of gravel
- 100 paving slabs
- 20 railway sleepers.

What is the truck's **total** loaded
weight in tonnes and kilograms?

5 (a) Find the total weight of the children in your class.

(b) How many kilograms more or less than 1 tonne is this total weight?

i X   3kg   0g   2kg   1kg

Y   0 kg   5 kg   10 kg

Z   200 g   100 g   0 g

Which of the scales X, Y or Z would be best
to use when weighing each of these items?

(a) SHAMPOO 150ml

(b) MILK 1 pint

(c) OLIVE OIL 5 litre

2 **Work in pairs.** For each activity:
- discuss how you could find the weight of the item
- weigh the item
- write about what you did.

A Find the weight of the teacher's chair.

B Find the weight of a container without emptying its contents. PEACHES

C Find the weight of one counter.

D Find the weight of a coat.

3 Use a two-pan balance, a 20 g weight
and a bag of cubes.
  (a) Weigh out 50 g of cubes in
     two **different** ways.
  (b) Write about each way.

1 Measure each bird in centimetres then calculate its true length.

Scale: 1 cm to 3 cm

(a) Firecrest

(b) Robin

(c) Goldfinch

(d) Little Grebe

(e) Sandpiper

2 Each bird is drawn to a different scale.

(a) Measure each wingspan in centimetres then calculate the length of the true wingspan.

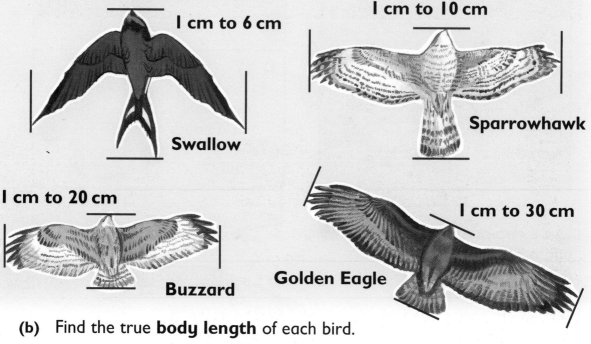

1 cm to 6 cm

1 cm to 10 cm

Swallow

Sparrowhawk

1 cm to 20 cm

1 cm to 30 cm

Buzzard

Golden Eagle

(b) Find the true **body length** of each bird.

1   This plan of the aviary is drawn to a scale of **1 cm to 2 m**.
    Find the true length and breadth of each part.

Eagles	
Parrots **Courtyard**	**Owls**
Exhibition Room	

2   These trees grow near the aviary.

(a) Find the true height of each tree.

Scots Pine	Yew	Rowan	Spruce	Elm
1 cm to 10 m	1 cm to 3 m	1 cm to 6 m	1 cm to 15 m	1 cm to 12 m

(b) Sketch each tree using a scale of **1 cm to 3 m**.

1 Which of these is likely to be the best estimate for each length?

| about 100 m | about 10 mm | about 1 m | about 1 km | about 10 m | about 100 km | about 10 cm | about 5 m |

length of
a belt

length of
a car

width of
a calculator

height of
a lamppost

length of an
airport runway

width of
a button

distance from
Newcastle to York

length of
a train

2 Which of these lengths would you measure in

(a) kilometres   **(b)** metres   **(c)** centimetres   **(d)** millimetres?

length of
a bus

height of
a tree

wingspan of
a midge

distance from the
Earth to the Moon

length of
a motorway

length of
a pencil

thickness of
a coin

height of
a house

3 Suggest two other items you would measure in

(a) kilometres   **(b)** metres   **(c)** centimetres   **(d)** millimetres.

1 Find the length of wood left when

(a) 35 cm is cut from the pine

(b) 1 m 65 cm is cut from the elm.

Pine
◀— 4 m —▶

Elm
◀——— 5½ m ———▶

2 Find the total length of wood used to make this section of fencing.

90 cm

◀— 1·3 m —▶

3

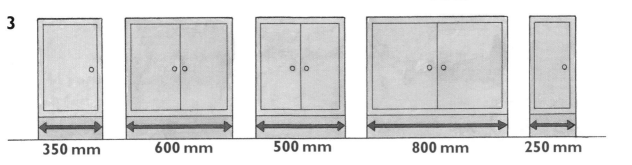

350 mm   600 mm   500 mm   800 mm   250 mm

(a) How wide are the cupboards each person should buy?

I need two cupboards with a total width of 140 cm.

I need three cupboards with a total width of 120 cm.

Dave

Senga

(b) Which four **different** cupboards have a total width of two metres?

4 Find the total distance travelled by Jim's van during the week.

Jim's Joinery Services

	Distance travelled
Monday	3 km
Tuesday	6700 m
Wednesday	4 km 450 m
Thursday	5·5 km
Friday	2800 m

1 Measure the perimeter of each shape.

(a)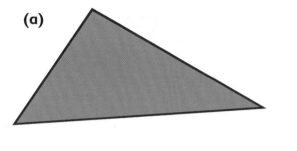

(b)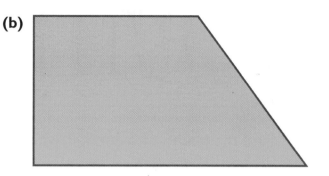

2 Calculate the perimeter of each shape.

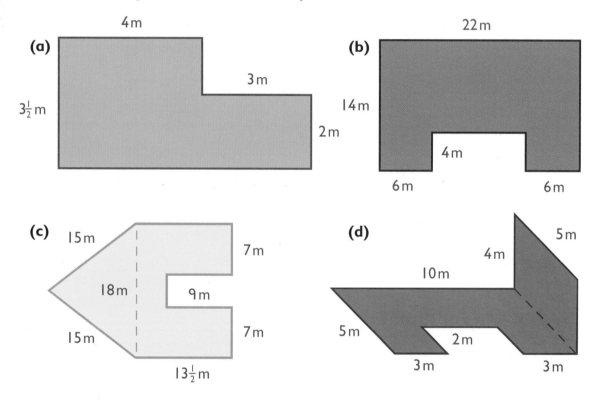

(a)

4m

$3\frac{1}{2}$ m

3m

2m

(b)

22m

14m

4m

6m   6m

(c)

15m

18m

15m

7m

9m

7m

$13\frac{1}{2}$ m

(d)

5m

4m

10m

5m

2m

3m   3m

3 Find the true perimeter of each building in these plans.

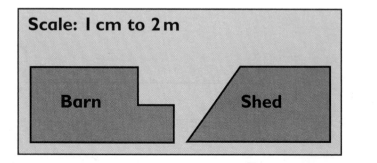

Scale: 1cm to 2m

Barn

Shed

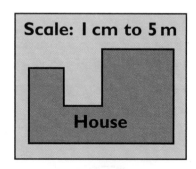

Scale: 1cm to 5m

House

1 **Measure** in millimetres to find the perimeter of each rectangle.

(a) **(b)** **(c)**

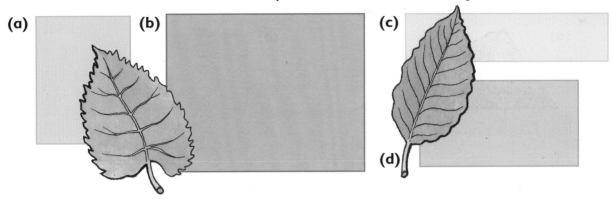

(d)

2 How can you calculate the perimeter of a rectangle when you know its length and breadth?

3 **Calculate** the perimeter of each rectangle.

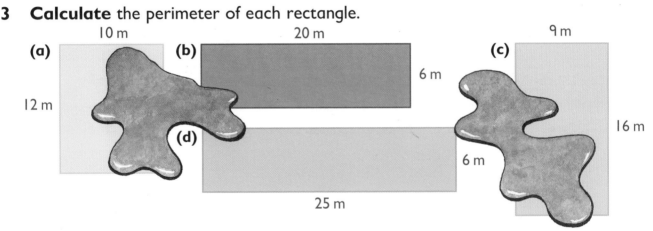

10 m **(a)** 20 m **(b)** 9 m **(c)**

12 m 6 m 16 m

(d) 6 m

25 m

4 New fencing is to be put up around the perimeter of each enclosure at City Farm. Calculate the length of fencing needed for

(a) the deer park - length 30 m, breadth 25 m
(b) the cow field - length 45 m, breadth 22 m
(c) the sheep pen - length 27 m, breadth 18 m.

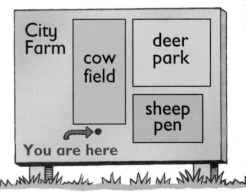

5 The City Farm
- is rectangular in shape
- is 65 metres long and 60 metres wide
- has a perimeter wall.

Calculate the length of the wall.

83

1 Write each time as a 24-hour time.

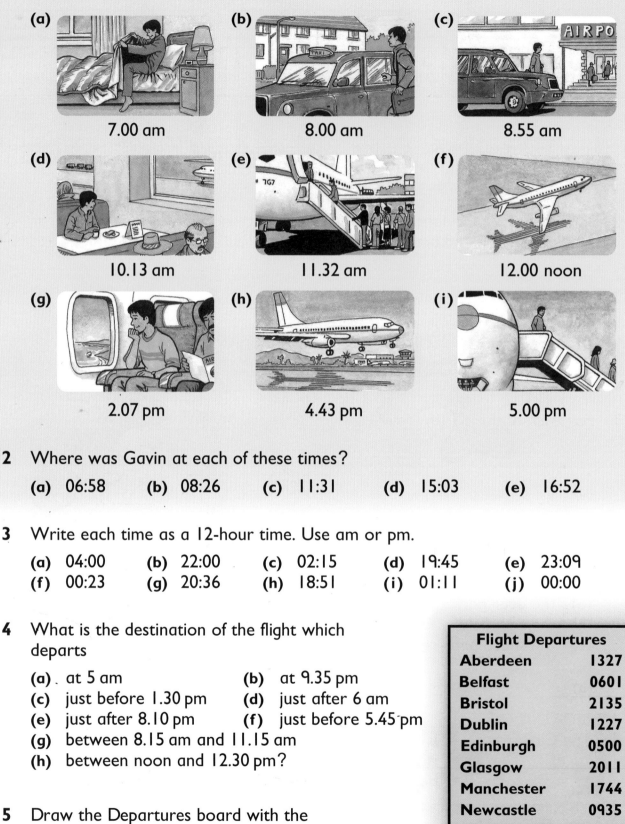

(a) 7.00 am   (b) 8.00 am   (c) 8.55 am

(d) 10.13 am   (e) 11.32 am   (f) 12.00 noon

(g) 2.07 pm   (h) 4.43 pm   (i) 5.00 pm

2 Where was Gavin at each of these times?

(a) 06:58   (b) 08:26   (c) 11:31   (d) 15:03   (e) 16:52

3 Write each time as a 12-hour time. Use am or pm.

(a) 04:00   (b) 22:00   (c) 02:15   (d) 19:45   (e) 23:09
(f) 00:23   (g) 20:36   (h) 18:51   (i) 01:11   (j) 00:00

4 What is the destination of the flight which departs

(a) at 5 am   (b) at 9.35 pm
(c) just before 1.30 pm   (d) just after 6 am
(e) just after 8.10 pm   (f) just before 5.45 pm
(g) between 8.15 am and 11.15 am
(h) between noon and 12.30 pm?

Flight Departures	
Aberdeen	1327
Belfast	0601
Bristol	2135
Dublin	1227
Edinburgh	0500
Glasgow	2011
Manchester	1744
Newcastle	0935

5 Draw the Departures board with the flights in order of take-off times.

Local Time Around the World

New York	Bermuda	London	Athens	Mumbai	Beijing	Adelaide
07:00	09:00	12:00	14:00	17:30	20:00	21:30

1 How many hours ahead of or behind the time in London is each local time?

2 When it is 14:30 in London what is the local time in

    (a) Athens   **(b)** Mumbai   **(c)** Bermuda?

3 For each of these local times, give the time in London.

Beijing	**Adelaide**	**New York**
(a) 23:00	**(b)** 17:30	**(c)** 06:00

4 The time in New York is 03:00. What is the local time in

    (a) Athens   **(b)** Bermuda   **(c)** Mumbai?

5 **(a)** A flight from London to Rome takes 3 hours. The flight takes off at 07:30. Local time in Rome is 1 hour ahead of London time. What is the local time when the plane lands in Rome?

    (b) Find the local landing time for each of these flights from London.

Destination	Cyprus	Moscow	Washington	San Francisco
Flying time	$4\frac{3}{4}$ h	$3\frac{1}{2}$ h	8 h	$11\frac{1}{2}$ h
Take-off time	09:00	09:45	14:00	17:30
Difference between local and London times	$^{+}2$ h	$^{+}4$ h	$^{-}5$ h	$^{-}8$ h

1 What is the time

(a)  15 minutes after... `10:50`

(b) 50 minutes later than... `12:35`

(c) 75 minutes later than... `17:25`

(d) 1 hour and 20 minutes after... `21:55`

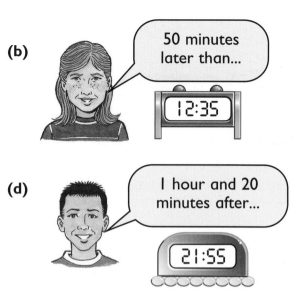

(e) 100 min later than 06:45

(f) 1h and 55 min after 22:40?

2 What is the time

(a) 25 minutes before... `07:15`

(b) 45 minutes earlier than... `10:05`

(c) 100 minutes earlier than... `19:40`

(d) 1 hour and 35 minutes before... `12:00`

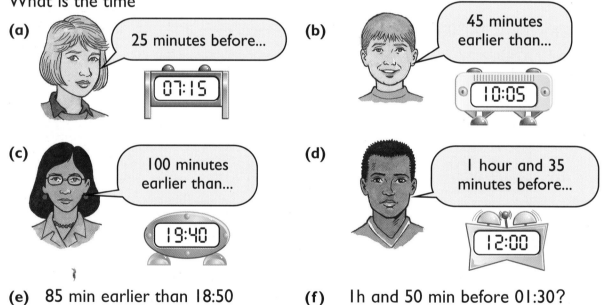

(e) 85 min earlier than 18:50

(f) 1h and 50 min before 01:30?

3 How many minutes are there between the **Start** and **Finish** times for each event?

24-hour Sport-a-thon	Start	Finish
(a) running	05:15	06:30
(b) jumping	08:25	09:55
(c) swimming	11:05	12:45

24-hour Sport-a-thon	Start	Finish
(d) cycling	13:10	15:00
(e) throwing	20:20	22:05
(f) walking	23:25	02:20

1

The Bruce family set out at 07:40. They arrived in the old town of Ambertini at 09:05. How long did their journey take?

2

They spent 85 minutes exploring Ambertini. At what time did they leave?

3

The journey from Ambertini to Cala took 65 minutes. At what time did the Bruce family arrive in Cala?

4

Mr and Mrs Bruce took a boat trip which left at 11:45 and lasted for 1 hour and 20 minutes. When did they arrive back in Cala?

5

Lucy and Harry went to the Water Sports Club from 11:35 to 13:20. How long did they spend at the club?

6

The family spent 1 hour and 55 minutes eating lunch then looking around Cala. They left Cala at 15:25. When did they start lunch?

7

The Bruce family arrived in Rivera for the Fiesta at 17:00. They returned to their holiday home at 23:10 after a 35 minute drive. How long did they spend at the Fiesta?

Train: Ambertini - Cala - Rivera

Dep	Ambertini	0710	1135	1550
Arr	Cala	0815	1250	1700
Dep	Cala	0820	1310	1715
Arr	Rivera	0915	1400	1820
Dep	Rivera	0925	1405	1825
Arr	Ambertini	1040	1535	1945

Boat: Cala - Bertoli

Dep	Cala	0905	1310	1740
Arr	Bertoli	0945	1400	1820
Dep	Bertoli	0955	1420	1835
Arr	Cala	1040	1505	1915

Boat: Rivera - Bertoli

Dep	Rivera	0920	1410	1830
Arr	Bertoli	0940	1435	1850
Dep	Bertoli	1010	1455	1905
Arr	Rivera	1035	1515	1935

1 The Bruce family travelled by train from Ambertini to Cala.
   The journey took 1 hour and 15 minutes. Which train did they catch?

2 The family took a boat from Cala to Bertoli and then another boat
   from Bertoli to Rivera. They arrived in Rivera at 15:15.
   How long did they spend in Bertoli?

3 (a) How long did they have to wait for a train back to Ambertini?
   (b) At what time did they arrive in Ambertini?

4 Is it possible to take a train from Ambertini to Cala, then go by boat
   to Rivera via Bertoli and travel back by train to Ambertini in time for
   tea at 16:15? Explain.

5 Lucy and Harry plan a day trip from
   Ambertini spending the time shown
   at the Gardens and at least two
   other places.

   Describe their journey.

30 min Gardens

1 h Bird Park

50 min Caves

45 min Fort

1 Copy and complete this table to show the cooking times.

Cooking time \ Weight	1 kg	1¼ kg	1½ kg	1¾ kg	2 kg	2¼ kg	2½ kg
Chicken	40 min						
Lamb	48 min						
Beef	60 min						

2 Cedric, the chef, is serving lunch at 1 pm.
What is the **latest** time he can start cooking

(a) 2 kg of chicken (b) $2\frac{1}{2}$ kg of beef

(c) $1\frac{3}{4}$ kg of lamb?

3 How long would you expect Cedric to take to
(a) boil an egg ⟶ 30 min **or** 15 min **or** 3 min?

(b) cook vegetable casserole ⟶ 1 hour **or** 3 hours **or** 6 hours?

(c) bake a fruit cake ⟶ $1\frac{1}{2}$ hours **or** 8 hours **or** 16 hours?

4

Cedric's break times	breakfast 20 min	morning coffee 15 min	lunch 35 min	dinner 1 h	supper 20 min

Cedric works for 5 days each week.
How much break time does he have altogether in 5 days?

5 Cleo, the assistant chef, is 21 years old.
Has she lived for more or less than
(a) 1000 weeks (b) 8000 days (c) 183 000 hours?

Explain.

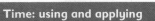

1 **Work with a partner**.

    (a) Write your age as often as you can in 10 seconds. Take turns to be the writer or the timer.

    (b) Calculate your **writing rate** in digits per second.

    (c) At this rate, how many digits could you write in
        • 1 minute   • 10 minutes   • 1 hour?

2 Calculate each rate.

    (a) Typing rate in letters per second.

    (b) Speaking rate in words per second.

    (c) Reading rate in words per second.

    Bill typed 60 letters in 30 seconds.

    Liz spoke 120 words in 20 seconds.

    Wes read 36 words in 15 seconds.

3 Sue sprinted 150 metres in 25 seconds. What was Sue's sprinting speed in metres per second?

4 Calculate each speed in metres per second.

    (a) Jan paddled 48 metres in 12 seconds.

    (b) Sal travelled 80 metres in 16 seconds.

    (c) Dec cycled 420 metres in 40 seconds.

5 **Work with a partner**.
Find your hopping speed in metres per second.

Cross-country run (24 miles)

The graph shows times taken to complete a 24-mile run.

(a) Who was the fastest runner?

(b) Calculate the average speed of each runner.

2 The *Queen Mary 2* cruised 225 miles in 9 hours. What was her speed in miles per hour?

3 Find each speed, in miles per hour, **to the nearest whole number**.

(a)

273 miles in 4 h

(b)

614 miles in 5 h

(c)

43 miles in 3 h

(d)

343 miles in 6 h

(e)

3500 miles in 8 h

(f)

274 miles in 14 h

4 The total length of Carla's journey was 130·5 miles.
She travelled by train for $2\frac{1}{4}$ hours at 54 miles per hour and then by bus for 24 minutes.

(a) How far did Carla travel by train?

(b) What was the average speed of the bus?

1 Write the capacity of each container
   • **in millilitres**

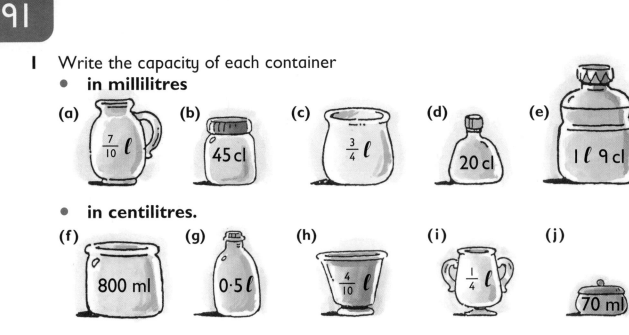

(a) $\frac{7}{10} \ell$ (b) 45 cl   (c) $\frac{3}{4} \ell$ (d) 20 cl   (e) 1 ℓ 9 cl

   • **in centilitres.**

(f) 800 ml   (g) 0·5 ℓ (h) $\frac{4}{10} \ell$ (i) $\frac{1}{4} \ell$ (j) 70 ml

2 What is the capacity of the container which
   • holds more

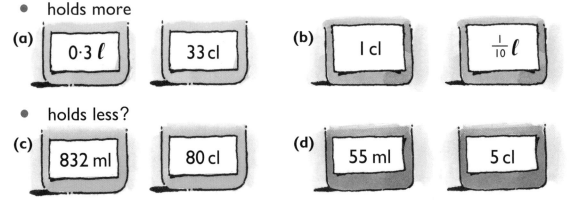

(a) 0·3 ℓ 33 cl   (b) 1 cl $\frac{1}{10} \ell$

   • holds less?

(c) 832 ml   80 cl   (d) 55 ml   5 cl

3 Write in order.

(a) Start with the **largest** volume.

| 66 cl | $\frac{6}{10} \ell$ | 6 ℓ | 606 ml | 6 cl |

(b) Start with the **smallest** volume.

| 13 ℓ | 1 ℓ 3 cl | 1·3 ℓ | 1003 ml | 133 cl |

4 Which of these containers have a capacity greater than 35 cl and
   smaller than 65 cl?

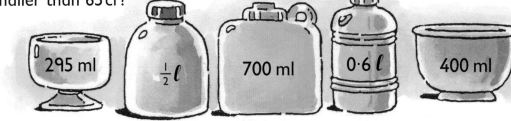

295 ml $\frac{1}{2} \ell$ 700 ml   0·6 ℓ 400 ml

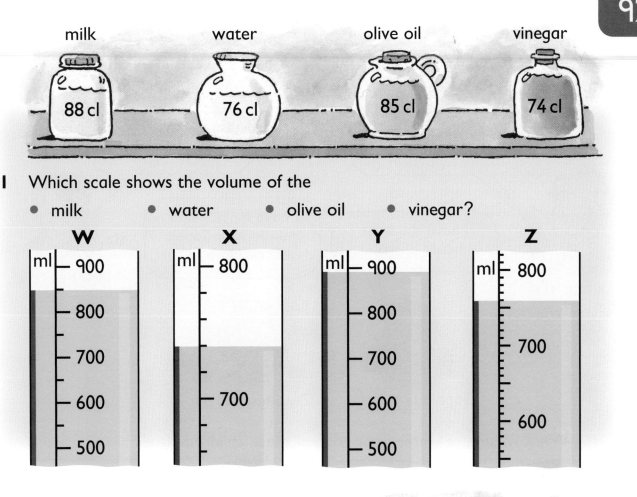

milk   water   olive oil   vinegar

88 cl   76 cl   85 cl   74 cl

1 Which scale shows the volume of the

- milk
- water
- olive oil
- vinegar?

2

For each container in turn
- estimate the capacity in centilitres
- check by measuring.

Record your results in a table like this.

Container	Estimate	Measure
A	about cl	about cl
B		

3 Find two other containers each with a capacity of between 35 cl and 0·5 ℓ.

1 Some children in Primary 7 have been pouring water into containers.

(a) Write True (T) or False (F) for each child's statement.

I have more water than Sophie but less than Zoe.

I have 50 cl more than Sophie.

I have the least amount of water.

I have more water than Jack or Sophie or Mark.

Mark has 95 cl.

Jack has 91 cl of water.

Sophie has $\frac{9}{10}\ell$.

Zoe has 940 ml.

(b) What volume of water does each of these children have?

I have 75 ml less than Mark.

Rosie

I have 10 cl more than Sophie.

Leela

2

1450 ml   1·1 ℓ 70 cl   360 ml   0·8 ℓ 30 cl

What is the total volume of paint in these containers?

(a) green and yellow
(b) brown and white
(c) blue and brown
(d) yellow and red
(e) red and green
(f) blue, yellow and white.

3

45 cl $\frac{4}{10}\ell$ 35 cl   50 cl   550 ml

The sum of which two volumes is
(a) 900 ml   (b) 0·75 ℓ (c) 1 ℓ 50 ml   (d) 1 ℓ?

Each cuboid is built using centimetre cubes.

1 Copy and complete the table.

Cuboid	Number of cubes in one row (length)	Number of rows (breadth)	Number of layers (height)	Volume in centimetre cubes
Yellow	6	4	3	cm³

2

Write a rule to find the volume of a cuboid when you know its length, breadth and height.

3 Find the volume, in cm³, of each of these cuboids.

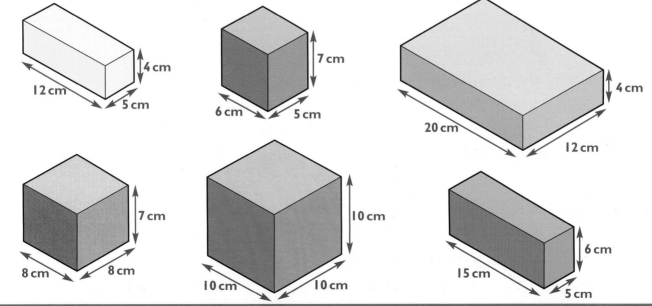

I litre is about 1¾ pints.

1 About how many **pints** of oxygen are in each tank?

(a) 2 ℓ   (b) 100 ℓ   (c) 12 ℓ   (d) 4½ ℓ

2 About how many **litres** are left in each fuel tank?

I gallon is about 4·5 litres.

(a)   (b)

10 gallons left   25 gallons left

(c)

150 gallons left

(d)

500 gallons left

3 I ounce is about 30 grams.

Write the approximate weight, **in grams,** of each moon rock.

(a) 4 ounces   (b) 7 ounces   (c) 12 ounces   (d) 10½ ounces

4 What is the approximate **total** weight, **in kilograms,** of these moon rocks?

300 g   4 ounces   250 g   11 ounces

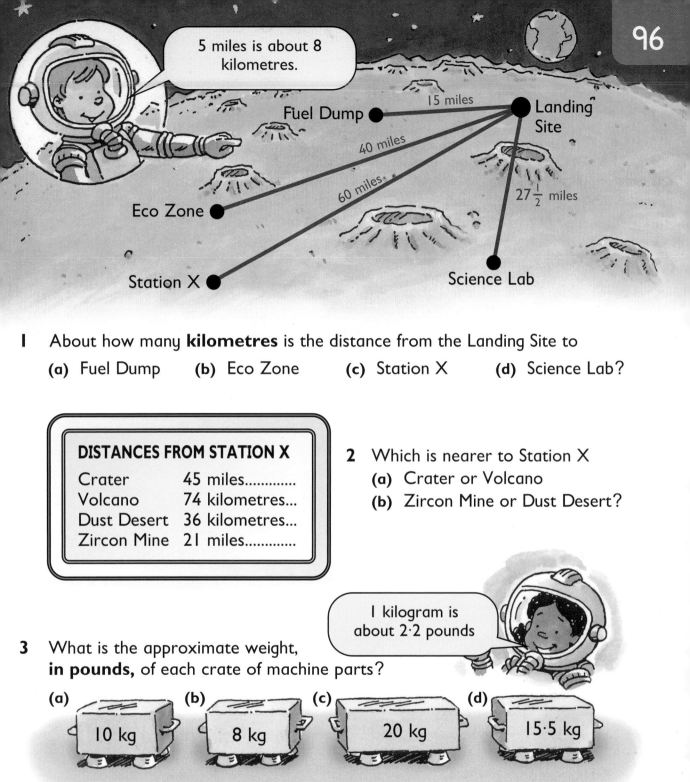

5 miles is about 8 kilometres.

Fuel Dump

15 miles — Landing Site

40 miles

60 miles

Eco Zone

$27\frac{1}{2}$ miles

Station X

Science Lab

1 About how many **kilometres** is the distance from the Landing Site to

(a) Fuel Dump   (b) Eco Zone   (c) Station X   (d) Science Lab?

DISTANCES FROM STATION X

Crater	45 miles.............
Volcano	74 kilometres...
Dust Desert	36 kilometres...
Zircon Mine	21 miles.............

2 Which is nearer to Station X
   (a) Crater or Volcano
   (b) Zircon Mine or Dust Desert?

1 kilogram is about 2·2 pounds

3 What is the approximate weight, **in pounds,** of each crate of machine parts?

(a) 10 kg   (b) 8 kg   (c) 20 kg   (d) 15·5 kg

4 List the Imperial **and** metric units which would be best for measuring

(a) the capacity of a tea pot
(b) the weight of a calculator
(c) the distance from the Earth to the Moon
(d) the capacity of a car's fuel tank
(e) the weight of a brick.

1 A square field has side lengths of
100 metres. What is the area of the field in
   (a) square metres   **(b)** hectares?

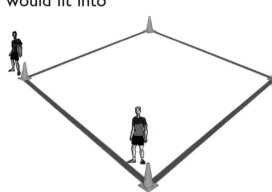

2 **(a)** Measure the length and breadth of your classroom.
  (b) Find the approximate area of your classroom in square metres.
  (c) About how many classrooms of this size would fit into
     an area of 1 hectare?

3 **(a)** Mark out a large square with side
     lengths of 25 m.
  (b) Find the area of the square in m^2.
  (c) How many squares of this size would
     fit into an area of 1 hectare?

4 A school football pitch has length 60 m and breadth 40 m.
About how many football pitches of this size would fit into
an area of 1 hectare?

5 **One hectare is represented by**

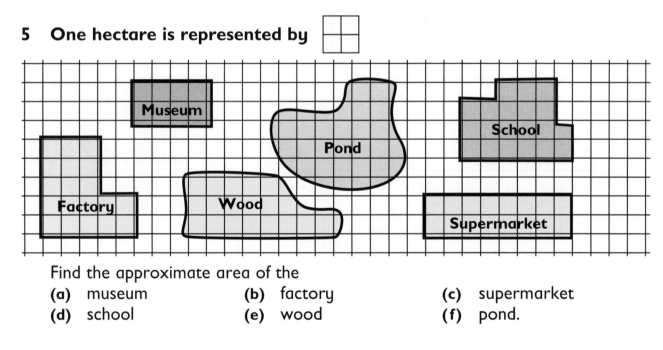

Find the approximate area of the
  (a) museum   **(b)** factory   **(c)** supermarket
  (d) school   **(e)** wood   **(f)** pond.

6 **(a)** How many square metres are in 1 square kilometre?
  (b) How many hectares are in 1 square kilometre?

7 About how many football pitches 60 metres long and 40 metres
broad would fit into an area of 1 square kilometre?

1 Calculate the area of each triangular sticker.

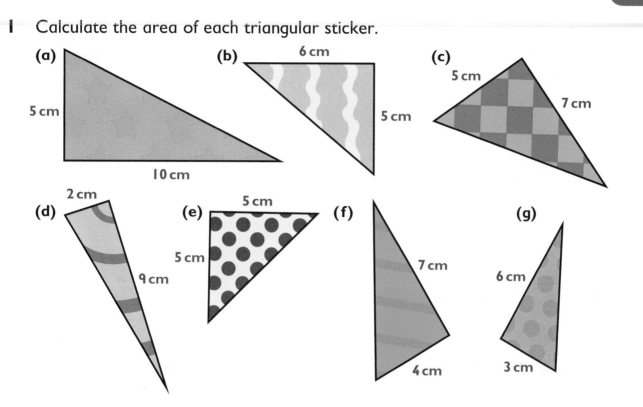

(a) 5 cm, 10 cm

(b) 6 cm, 5 cm

(c) 5 cm, 7 cm

(d) 2 cm, 9 cm

(e) 5 cm, 5 cm

(f) 7 cm, 4 cm

(g) 6 cm, 3 cm

2 Calculate the area of each design.

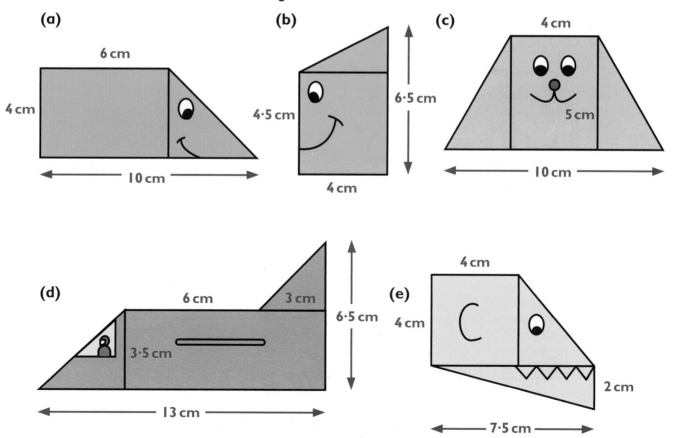

(a) 6 cm, 4 cm, 10 cm

(b) 4·5 cm, 6·5 cm, 4 cm

(c) 4 cm, 5 cm, 10 cm

(d) 6 cm, 3 cm, 6·5 cm, 3·5 cm, 13 cm

(e) 4 cm, 4 cm, 2 cm, 7·5 cm

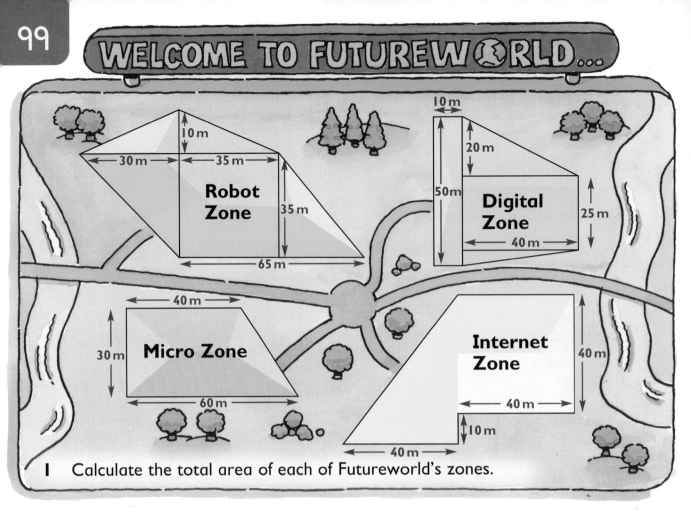

WELCOME TO FUTUREW🌐RLD...

1 Calculate the total area of each of Futureworld's zones.

2 For each shape, measure side or other lengths then calculate the area.

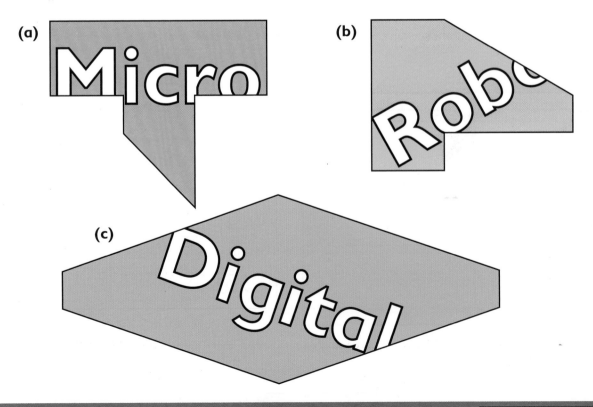

(a)

(b)

(c)

1 (a) Make each of these shapes.

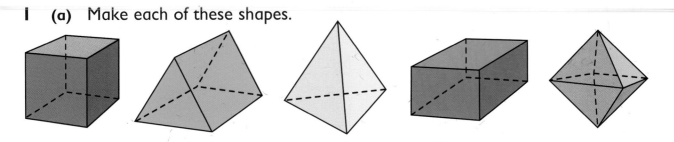

(b) Copy and complete this table for your shapes.

Shape	Number of faces	Number of vertices	Number of edges
Cube			

(c) Look for a pattern in your table.
Write a rule to find the number of edges when you
know the number of faces and vertices.

2 (a) Use your rule from question 1 to complete this
information for a square pyramid.

Square pyramid	5		8

(b) Construct a square pyramid to check.

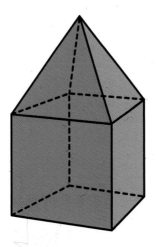

3 (a) Extend your table for this
'tower' shape.

(b) Construct the shape to check,
if you need to.

4 What is the **total** length of the edges of a cube whose faces each have an
area of 9 cm^2?

1 Name each shape.

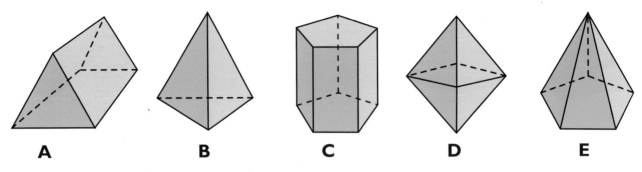

| A | B | C | D | E |

2 Match each shape from question **1** to its net.

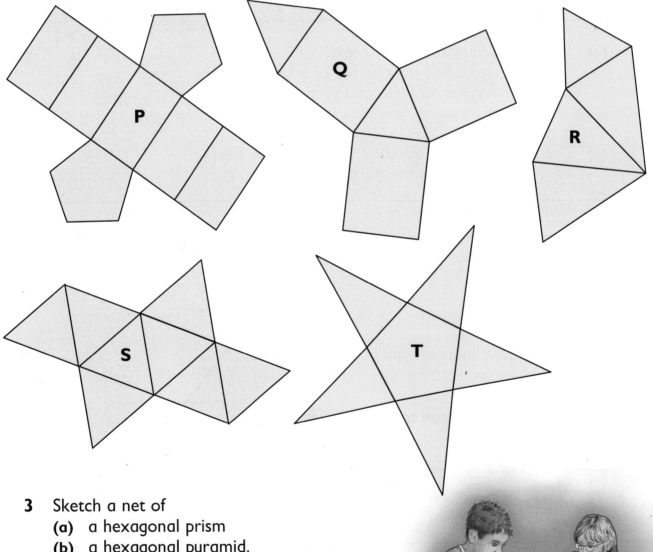

3 Sketch a net of
(a) a hexagonal prism
(b) a hexagonal pyramid.

Check, if you need to, by making the net and
the shape.

1 Use squared paper. For each shape, draw the
- plan view
- front view
- side view.

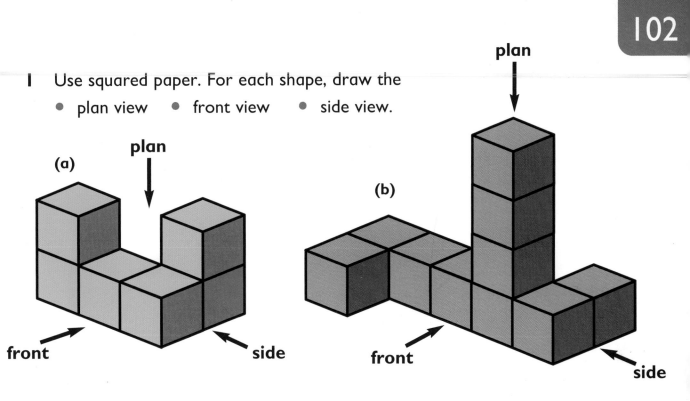

2 Sketch the plan view of each shape.

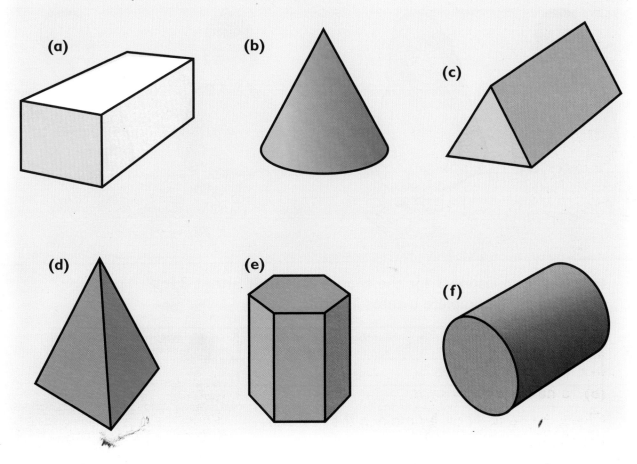

1 (a) Cut out the shapes from the bottom half of **Pupil Sheet 30**.
(b) Rotate each shape on top of its twin from the top half.
(c) Write on each shape the number of times it fits its outline
    in one complete turn.
(d) Stick the shapes in your exercise book.

2

(a) Repeat question 1 for the shapes on **Pupil Sheet 31**.
(b) Copy and complete a table like this:

Regular polygon	Number of equal sides and equal angles	Number of times it fits its outline
Equilateral triangle	3	3

(c) What do you notice?

1 **(a)** Copy each design on squared paper.

(b) Complete each design so that it has rotational symmetry.

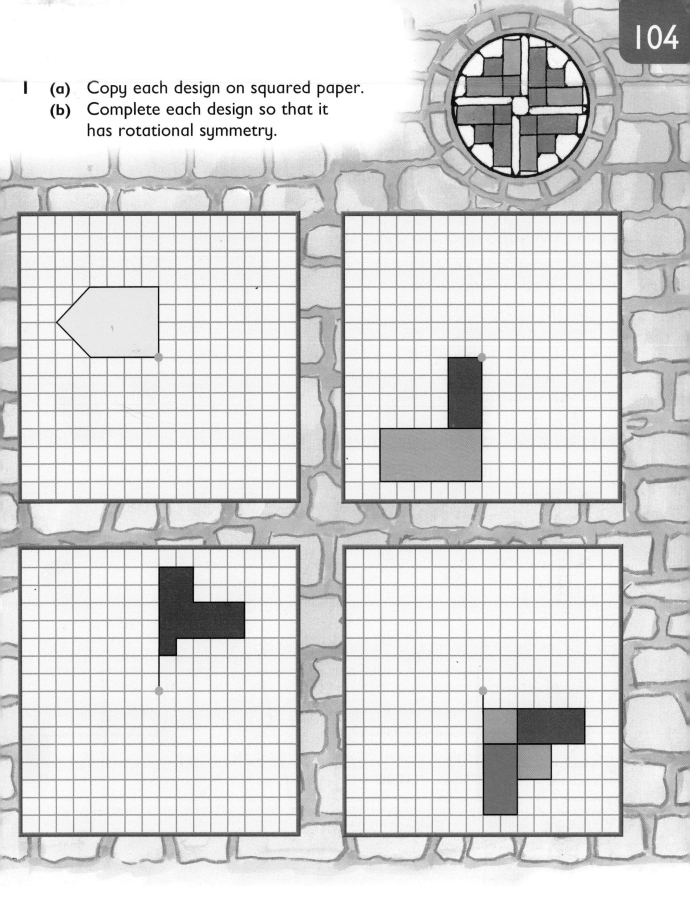

2 Draw and colour designs of your own that have rotational symmetry.

1 In which shapes is the red line a diagonal?

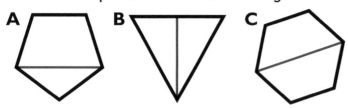

You need two long and two short strips.

2 Use one long and one short strip as diagonals of a quadrilateral.

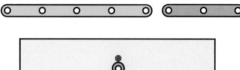

- Join the strips as shown.
- Mark the ends of each diagonal.
- What shape do you think is made when the ends are joined by straight lines?
- Check by drawing the lines.

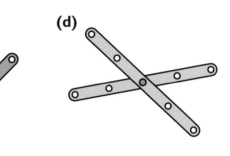

3 Repeat question **2** with strips joined like these.

(a) **(b)** **(c)** **(d)**

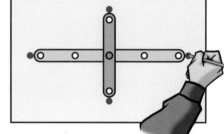

4 **(a)** Draw these diagonals on squared paper.

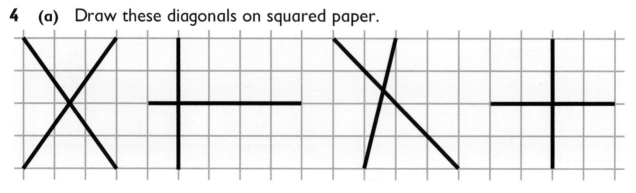

(b) What shapes do you think are made when the ends of the diagonals are joined by straight lines?
Check by drawing the lines.

(c) Name the quadrilaterals with diagonals that
- intersect at right angles
- are **not** the same length.

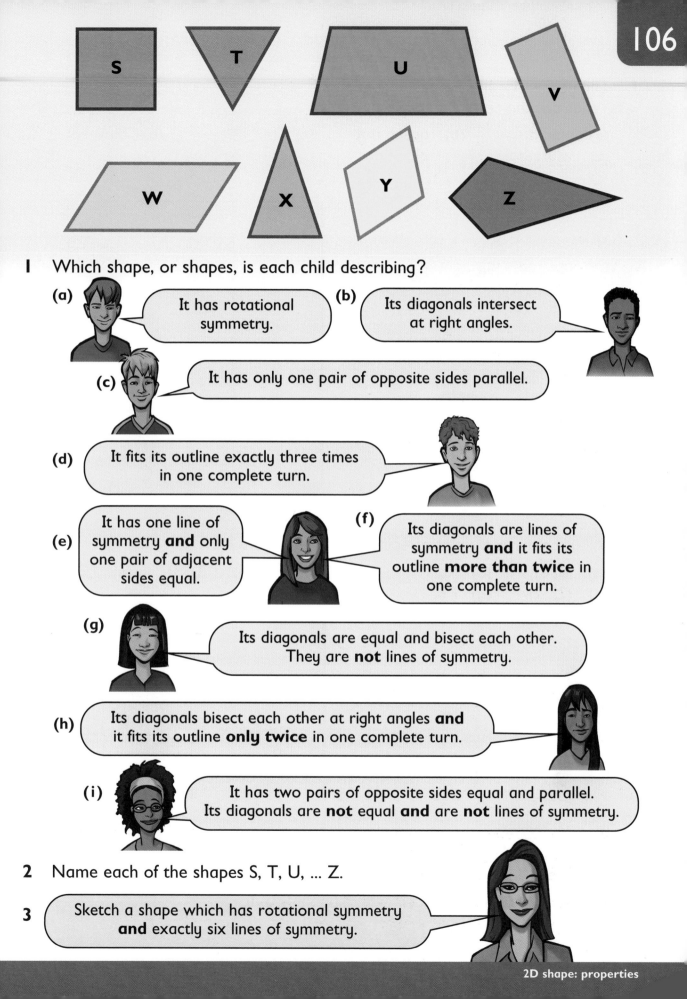

1 Which shape, or shapes, is each child describing?

(a) It has rotational symmetry.

(b) Its diagonals intersect at right angles.

(c) It has only one pair of opposite sides parallel.

(d) It fits its outline exactly three times in one complete turn.

(e) It has one line of symmetry **and** only one pair of adjacent sides equal.

(f) Its diagonals are lines of symmetry **and** it fits its outline **more than twice** in one complete turn.

(g) Its diagonals are equal and bisect each other. They are **not** lines of symmetry.

(h) Its diagonals bisect each other at right angles **and** it fits its outline **only twice** in one complete turn.

(i) It has two pairs of opposite sides equal and parallel. Its diagonals are **not** equal **and** are **not** lines of symmetry.

2 Name each of the shapes S, T, U, ... Z.

3 Sketch a shape which has rotational symmetry **and** exactly six lines of symmetry.

1 The yellow dot has co-ordinates (⁻4, 2).
What are the co-ordinates of the

(a) pink dot   **(b)** green dot   **(c)** red dot   **(d)** blue dot
(e) white dot   **(f)** black dot   **(g)** orange dot?

2 What colour is the dot at each of these positions?

(a) (3, 3)   **(b)** (0, 1)   **(c)** (6, ⁻1)   **(d)** (⁻3, ⁻3)   **(e)** (⁻5, 0)
(f) (2, ⁻2)   **(g)** (⁻6, 1)   **(h)** (0, 0)

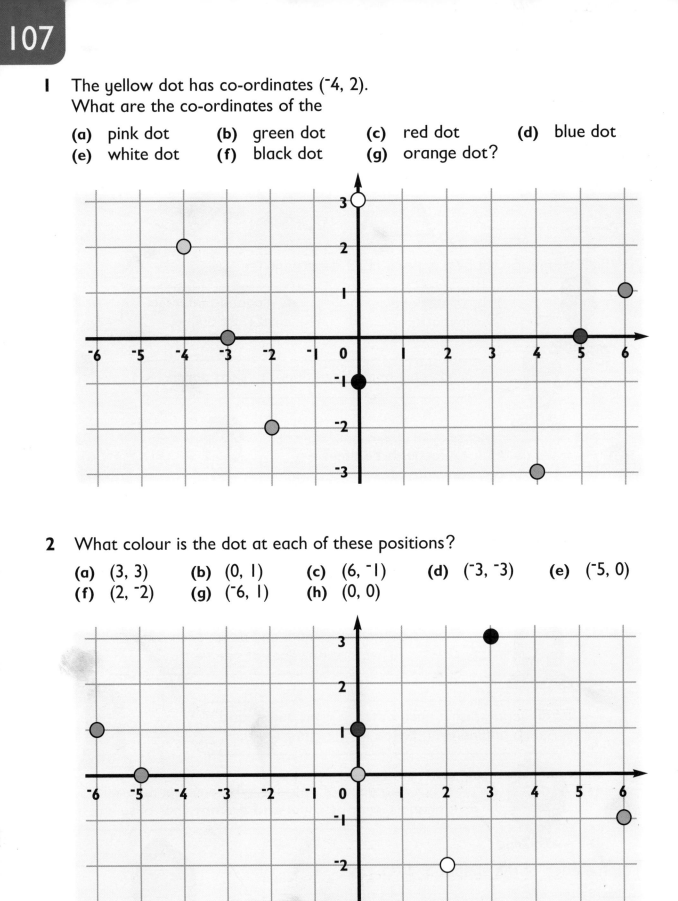

Trace each shape then flip to find reflections.

1   List the co-ordinates of
   - the vertices of the half shape
   - the vertices needed to complete the shape so that
     the **horizontal** axis is a line of symmetry.

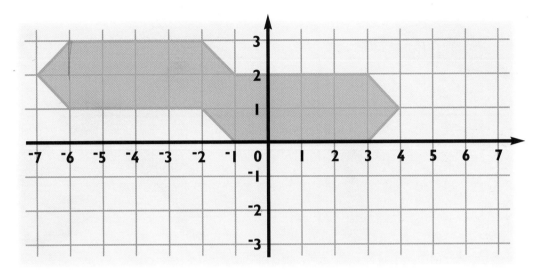

2   List the co-ordinates of
   - the vertices of the shape
   - the vertices of the shape's reflections when the
     horizontal **and** vertical axes are lines of symmetry.

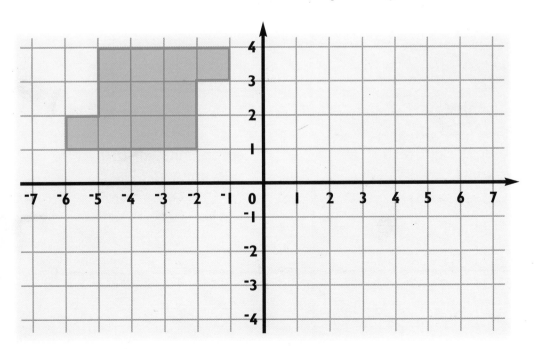

Use tracing paper if you need to.

1 List the co-ordinates of the vertices of each shape
  - in the position shown
  - after the shape has moved

(a) six units right

(b) five units left

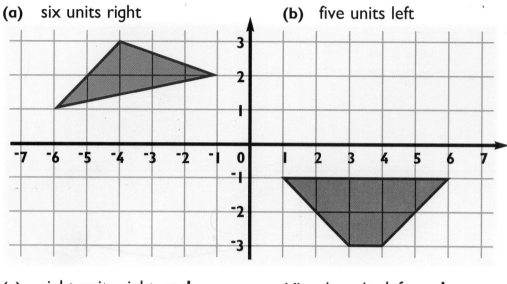

(c) eight units right **and** one unit up

(d) six units left **and** two units down

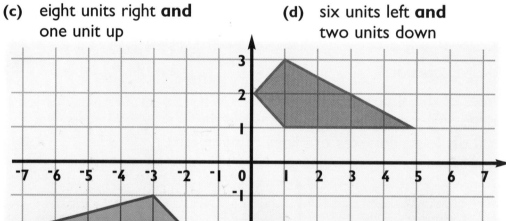

(e) five units right **and** two units down

(f) seven units left **and** two units up.

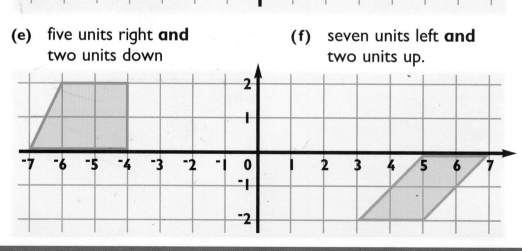

Trace each shape and rotate to find its new position.

I List the co-ordinates of the vertices of each shape

- in the position shown
- after the shape has rotated about the vertex at (0, 0)

(a) 90° anti-clockwise

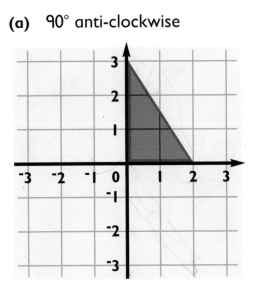

(b) 180° clockwise

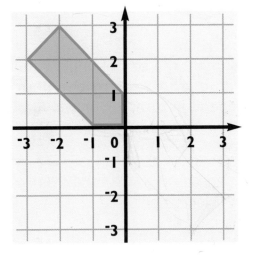

(c) 90° clockwise

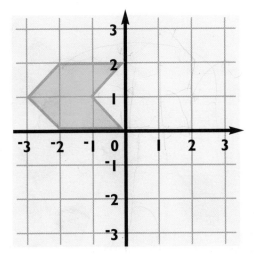

(d) 180° anti-clockwise.

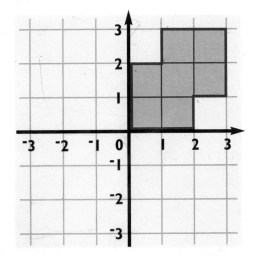

1 Which angles are   ● acute   ● obtuse   ● reflex?

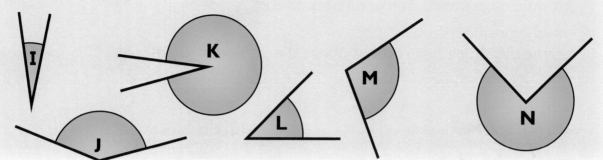

2 **(a)** Estimate the size of angle **P** then check by measuring
      with a protractor **to the nearest degree**.
   (b) Repeat, in turn, for angles **Q**, **R**, **S**, **T** and **U**.

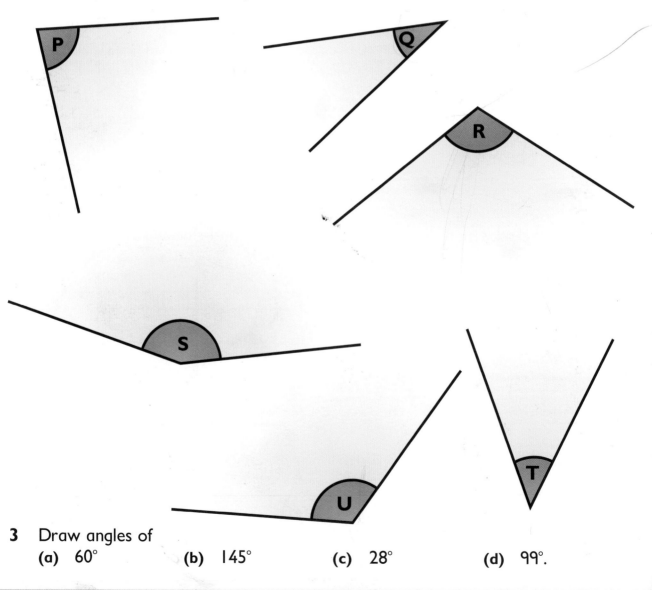

3 Draw angles of
   (a) 60°   **(b)** 145°   **(c)** 28°   **(d)** 99°.

1 Calculate the size of each red angle.

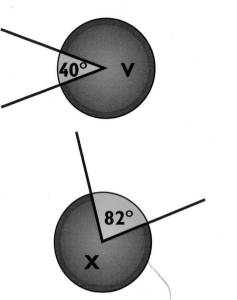

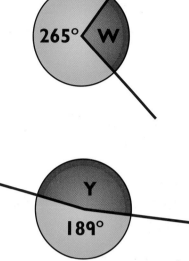

2 Calculate the size of each blue angle.

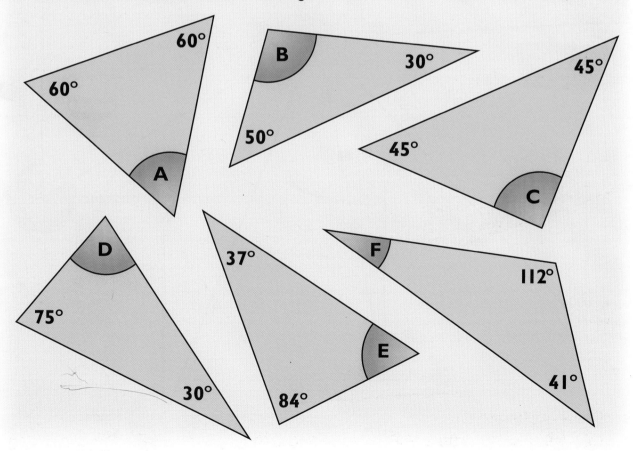

I Write the bearing of the Castle from each feature.

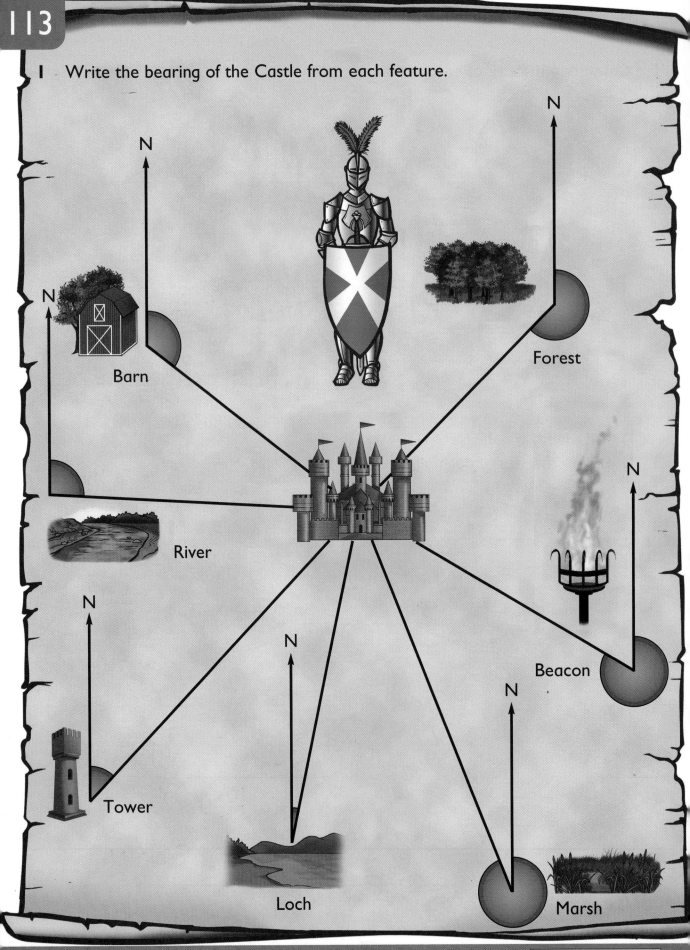

Work as a group.

1 You are going to carry out a survey of your class to find out who has a pet **and** what kind of pet they have.

(a) Which of these questionnaires would be better to use? Explain.

Pet	Number of pets	Total
Goldfish	⊥⊥⊥⊥ I	
Rabbit	I I	
Hamster	I I I	

Dog	Cat	Gerbil
Jake Alan	Mina Robbie(2)	Emma (3) Rosie
Total ☐	Total ☐	Total ☐

(b) Carry out the survey using the questionnaire you think is better.

(c) Draw a graph to show your results.

(d) Write a short report about what you have found.

> The most popular pet was...

> More girls than boys owned a...

2 (a) Design your own questionnaire and carry out a survey to find which one of these 'impossible pets' each child in your class would choose to have.

- Tarantula
- Python
- Crocodile
- Panda
- Piranha fish
- Tiger
- Vulture

(b) Make a display of your results.

(c) Write a short report about what you have found.

115

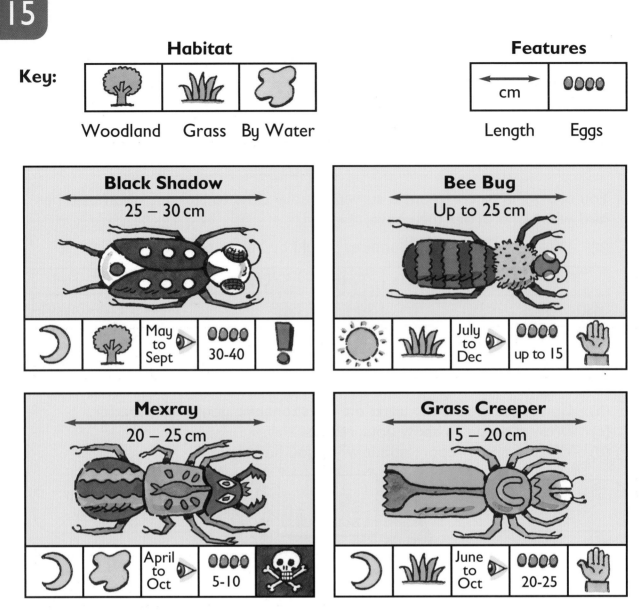

Key:

Habitat

Woodland   Grass   By Water

Features

cm

Length   Eggs

Black Shadow
25 – 30 cm

May to Sept   30-40

Bee Bug
Up to 25 cm

July to Dec   up to 15

Mexray
20 – 25 cm

April to Oct   5-10

Grass Creeper
15 – 20 cm

June to Oct   20-25

1   Use the information from the insect database to complete Pupil Sheet 37.

2   During which months is it possible to see   **(a)** all the insects
  (b) **only** three types of insects?

3   **(a)**   Which woodland insect that feeds in daytime can be handled safely?
  (b)   Which insect, seen in April, feeds at night-time and is poisonous?
  (c)   Which insect, seen in May, lives in woodland and feeds in daytime?

4   Which insect

  (a)   •   is found in woodland   **(b)**   •   feeds at night
       •   could be 30 cm long   •   can be handled safely
       •   can be seen in June   •   lays fewer than 30 eggs?

Danger Level

Poisonous	Bites	Safe

Feeds

Daytime	Night-time

Active

Months

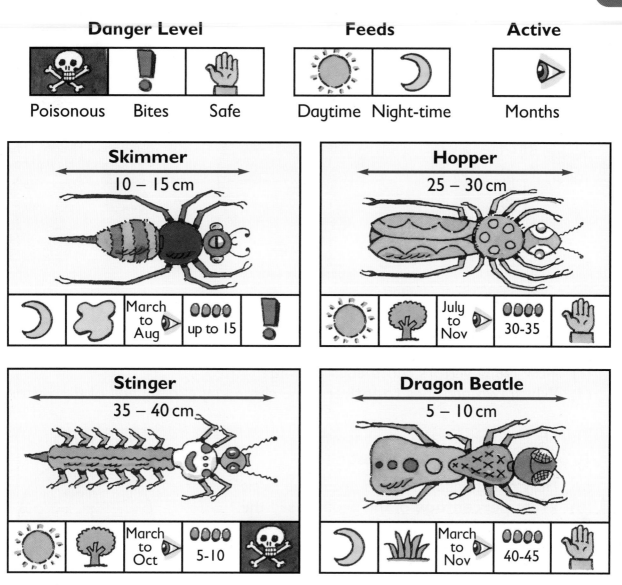

Skimmer
10 – 15 cm
March to Aug · up to 15

Hopper
25 – 30 cm
July to Nov · 30-35

Stinger
35 – 40 cm
March to Oct · 5-10

Dragon Beatle
5 – 10 cm
March to Nov · 40-45

5 Find the insect that

(a)
- can be seen in September
- lays more than 10 eggs
- feeds at night
- lives in grassland
- could be 10 cm long

(b)
- is active for less than 9 months
- might lay more than 10 eggs
- could be 25 cm in length
- lives in grassland
- feeds during the daytime.

6 Write two clues to find only the **Skimmer**.

7 Ask your teacher if you can enter the information into a computer database.

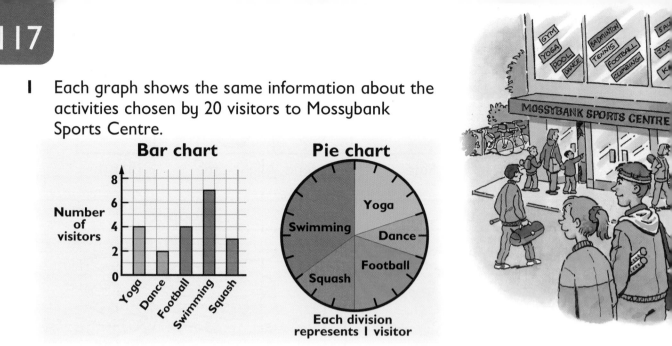

1 Each graph shows the same information about the activities chosen by 20 visitors to Mossybank Sports Centre.

Find each answer and write which graph shows it more clearly.

(a) Which activity did more than one quarter of the visitors choose?
(b) Which two activities were chosen by the same number of visitors?
(c) How many visitors chose each activity?
(d) Which two activities **together** were chosen by exactly half of the visitors?

2 The pie chart shows the seasons when 10 people used the Centre most often.

(a) How many equal divisions are in the circle?
(b) What **percentage** of the people used the Centre most often in • Spring • Autumn?
(c) In which season was the Centre used most often by exactly
   • 20% of the people • 40% of the people?

Seasonal Use

3 The pie chart shows how many times 100 people visited the Centre in June.

(a) What were the most common and the least common numbers of visits?
(b) How many equal divisions are in the circle?
(c) What **percentage** of the people visited the Centre
   • twice • more than four times
   • fewer than three times
   • more than once
   • **between** one and five times?

Number of visits: June

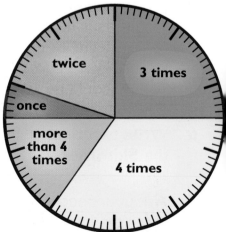

4 Show the information in the pie chart as a **bar line** chart.

Class 7 carried out a survey to find out how far children can 'kangaroo jump'.

Kangaroo jumps

1 Which class interval contains

(a) the greatest number of children
(b) the smallest number of children?

2 In which class interval is

(a) the shortest jump
(b) the longest jump?

3 How many children altogether took part in the kangaroo jump?

4 How many children jumped

(a) further than 119 cm   (b) less than 160 cm?

5 What **fraction** of the children jumped

(a) less than 140 cm   (b) between 119 cm and 180 cm?

6 What **percentage** of the children jumped further than 139 cm?

7

> Forty percent of the children in Year 6 can kangaroo jump further than 139 cm.

Use **Pupil Sheet 39** and the data below to find out if this is true by

- completing the frequency table
- drawing a bar chart.

Year 6 kangaroo jumps (cm)									
113	123	165	121	125	107	130	115	128	118
145	136	174	142	150	158	145	116	136	147
124	156	106	180	127	137	113	152	140	109
114	136	173	125	132	116	109	159	169	153
108	140	134	183	106	153	139	124	148	132

This straight-line graph shows the relationship between Pounds (£) and Euros (€) in 2003.

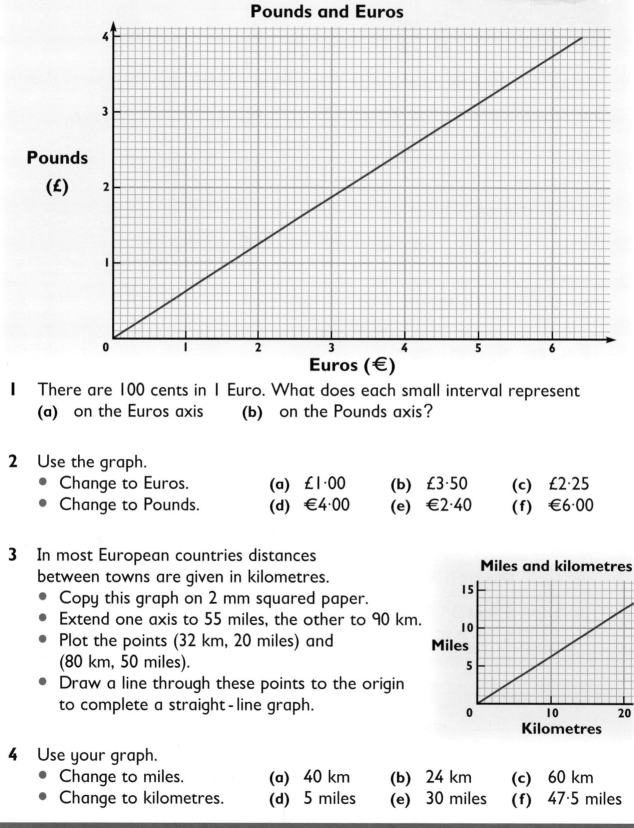

Pounds and Euros

Pounds (£)

Euros (€)

1 There are 100 cents in 1 Euro. What does each small interval represent
   (a) on the Euros axis   **(b)** on the Pounds axis?

2 Use the graph.
   • Change to Euros.   **(a)** £1·00   **(b)** £3·50   **(c)** £2·25
   • Change to Pounds.   **(d)** €4·00   **(e)** €2·40   **(f)** €6·00

3 In most European countries distances between towns are given in kilometres.
   • Copy this graph on 2 mm squared paper.
   • Extend one axis to 55 miles, the other to 90 km.
   • Plot the points (32 km, 20 miles) and (80 km, 50 miles).
   • Draw a line through these points to the origin to complete a straight-line graph.

   Miles and kilometres

   Miles

   Kilometres

4 Use your graph.
   • Change to miles.   **(a)** 40 km   **(b)** 24 km   **(c)** 60 km
   • Change to kilometres.   **(d)** 5 miles **(e)** 30 miles **(f)** 47·5 miles

1 Find the area, in cm², of each right-angled isosceles triangle.

If you need to, draw the triangles on centimetre squared paper.

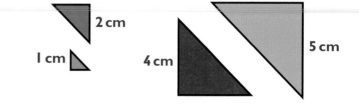

2 The graph shows the relationship between the length of the equal sides and the area, for right-angled isosceles triangles.

Use the graph.

(a) Check your answers to question **1**.

(b) What is the area of the triangle when the lengths of the equal sides are
- 6 cm
- 7 cm?

(c) What are the lengths of the equal sides when the area of the triangle is
- 32 cm²
- $4\frac{1}{2}$ cm²?

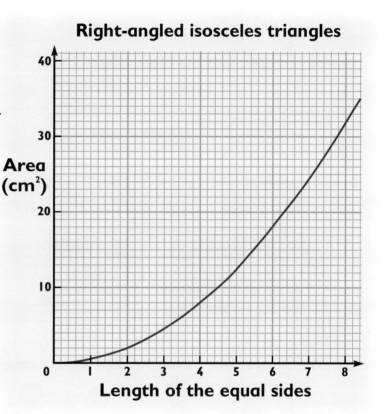

Right-angled isosceles triangles

Area (cm²)

Length of the equal sides

3 **(a)** Copy this **Square numbers** graph on 2 mm squared paper.

(b) Extend one axis to 10 and the other to 100.

(c) Plot these points:
(1, 1), (2, 4), (3, 9), (4, 16),… (10, 100).

(d) Draw a line through the points to the origin to complete a smooth curved-line graph.

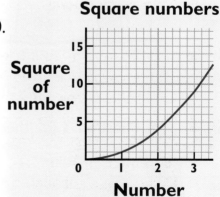

Square numbers

Square of number

Number

4 Use your graph.

(a) What number, **approximately**,
- is the square of 4·5
- has 56·25 as its square?

(b) Use a calculator to check your answers to part **(a)**.

Four schools took part in a fun day.

1 The points scored in the keepie-uppie competition
by the members of the Comrie team were

6   8   13   7   15   3   8   9   5   17   8

(a) For the Comrie team's points, find
● the range   ● the mode   ● the median.

(b) Find the mean number of points scored by dividing the total
number of points by the number of children in the team.

2 For each of these schools' points in the keepie-uppie competition, find
(a) the range   **(b)** the mode   **(c)** the median   **(d)** the mean.

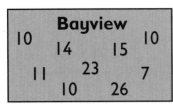

Bayview

10   14   15   10   11   23   7   10   26

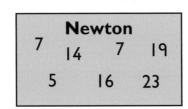

Newton

7   14   7   19   5   16   23

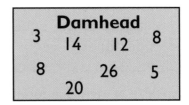

Damhead

3   14   12   8   8   26   5   20

3 The times taken, in seconds, by the Newton team for the sack race were:

26   28   33   25   34   29   28

For the Newton team's times, find
(a) the range   **(b)** the mode   **(c)** the median   **(d)** the mean.

4 Repeat question **3** for these schools' sack race times.

Comrie

19   21   18   22   18   21   17   23   18   24   19

Bayview

25   30   31   29   26   26   31   28   26

Damhead

36   23   25   27   35   29   34   23

1 Your class is going on a trip to the seashore.

Use | impossible | **or** | unlikely | **or** | likely | **or** | certain |

to describe the likelihood of each of these events happening.

(a) You will see a crab.

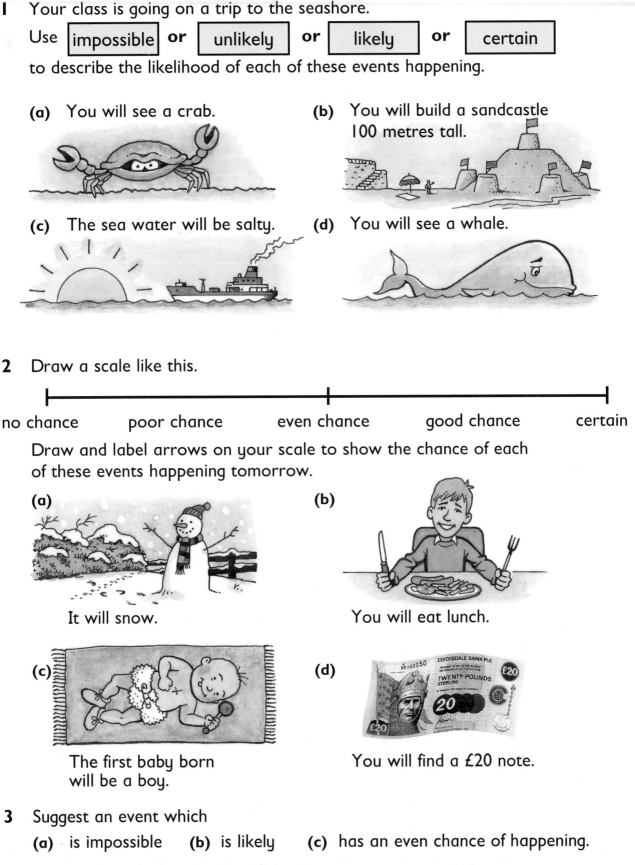

(b) You will build a sandcastle 100 metres tall.

(c) The sea water will be salty.

(d) You will see a whale.

2 Draw a scale like this.

no chance   poor chance   even chance   good chance   certain

Draw and label arrows on your scale to show the chance of each of these events happening tomorrow.

(a)

It will snow.

(b)

You will eat lunch.

(c)

The first baby born will be a boy.

(d)

You will find a £20 note.

3 Suggest an event which

(a) is impossible   **(b)** is likely   **(c)** has an even chance of happening.

School Fair

1 List all the possible outcomes if the arrow sticks to a card with

    (a) an odd number
    (b) a multiple of 4
    (c) a square number
    (d) a prime number.

2 List all the possible outcomes if the fish caught shows

    (a) an even number
    (b) a multiple of 3
    (c) a factor of 12
    (d) a triangular number.

3 What is the probability of rolling a die to give

    (a) a two
    (b) an odd number
    (c) a number less than 5
    (d) a number between 0 and 10?

4 Sally sells one hundred raffle tickets numbered 1 to 100.

Use ⬚ less than one in two ⬚ or ⬚ one in two ⬚ or ⬚ more than one in two ⬚

to describe the probability of each of these events happening.

    (a) The winning ticket is a multiple of 5.
    (b) The winning ticket is an even number.

TOPIC ASSESSMENT